CORAZON
AQUINO

CORAZON AQUINO

Howard Chua-Eoan

Macmillan/McGraw-Hill School Publishing Company
New York ▪ Chicago ▪ Columbus

For information regarding permission, write to Chelsea House
Publishers, 1974 Sproul Road, Suite 400, Broomall, PA 19008.

This edition is reprinted by arrangement with Chelsea House
Publishers, a division of Main Line Book Co.

Cover illustration: Kye Carbone

Macmillan/McGraw-Hill School Division
10 Union Square East
New York, New York 10003

Printed in the United States of America
ISBN 0-02-179539-8 / 7, L.13A
1 2 3 4 5 6 7 8 9 WES 99 98 97 96 95 94 93 92

Contents

John Adams
John Quincy Adams
Konrad Adenauer
Alexander the Great
Salvador Allende
Marc Antony
Corazon Aquino
Yasir Arafat
King Arthur
Hafez al-Assad
Kemal Atatürk
Attila
Clement Attlee
Augustus Caesar
Menachem Begin
David Ben-Gurion
Otto von Bismarck
Léon Blum
Simon Bolívar
Cesare Borgia
Willy Brandt
Leonid Brezhnev
Julius Caesar
John Calvin
Jimmy Carter
Fidel Castro
Catherine the Great
Charlemagne
Chiang Kai-Shek
Winston Churchill
Georges Clemenceau
Cleopatra
Constantine the Great
Hernán Cortés
Oliver Cromwell
Georges-Jacques
  Danton
Jefferson Davis
Moshe Dayan
Charles de Gaulle
Eamon De Valera
Eugene Debs
Deng Xiaoping
Benjamin Disraeli
Alexander Dubček
François & Jean-Claude
  Duvalier
Dwight Eisenhower
Eleanor of Aquitaine
Elizabeth I
Faisal
Ferdinand & Isabella
Francisco Franco
Benjamin Franklin

Frederick the Great
Indira Gandhi
Mohandas Gandhi
Giuseppe Garibaldi
Amin & Bashir Gemayel
Genghis Khan
William Gladstone
Mikhail Gorbachev
Ulysses S. Grant
Ernesto "Che" Guevara
Tenzin Gyatso
Alexander Hamilton
Dag Hammarskjöld
Henry VIII
Henry of Navarre
Paul von Hindenburg
Hirohito
Adolf Hitler
Ho Chi Minh
King Hussein
Ivan the Terrible
Andrew Jackson
James I
Wojciech Jaruzelski
Thomas Jefferson
Joan of Arc
Pope John XXIII
Pope John Paul II
Lyndon Johnson
Benito Juárez
John Kennedy
Robert Kennedy
Jomo Kenyatta
Ayatollah Khomeini
Nikita Khrushchev
Kim Il Sung
Martin Luther King, Jr.
Henry Kissinger
Kublai Khan
Lafayette
Robert E. Lee
Vladimir Lenin
Abraham Lincoln
David Lloyd George
Louis XIV
Martin Luther
Judas Maccabeus
James Madison
Nelson & Winnie
  Mandela
Mao Zedong
Ferdinand Marcos
George Marshall

Mary, Queen of Scots
Tomáš Masaryk
Golda Meir
Klemens von Metternich
James Monroe
Hosni Mubarak
Robert Mugabe
Benito Mussolini
Napoléon Bonaparte
Gamal Abdel Nasser
Jawaharlal Nehru
Nero
Nicholas II
Richard Nixon
Kwame Nkrumah
Daniel Ortega
Mohammed Reza Pahlavi
Thomas Paine
Charles Stewart
  Parnell
Pericles
Juan Perón
Peter the Great
Pol Pot
Muammar el-Qaddafi
Ronald Reagan
Cardinal Richelieu
Maximilien Robespierre
Eleanor Roosevelt
Franklin Roosevelt
Theodore Roosevelt
Anwar Sadat
Haile Selassie
Prince Sihanouk
Jan Smuts
Joseph Stalin
Sukarno
Sun Yat-sen
Tamerlane
Mother Teresa
Margaret Thatcher
Josip Broz Tito
Toussaint L'Ouverture
Leon Trotsky
Pierre Trudeau
Harry Truman
Queen Victoria
Lech Walesa
George Washington
Chaim Weizmann
Woodrow Wilson
Xerxes
Emiliano Zapata
Zhou Enlai

ON LEADERSHIP

Arthur M. Schlesinger, jr.

LEADERSHIP, it may be said, is really what makes the world go round. Love no doubt smooths the passage; but love is a private transaction between consenting adults. Leadership is a public transaction with history. The idea of leadership affirms the capacity of individuals to move, inspire, and mobilize masses of people so that they act together in pursuit of an end. Sometimes leadership serves good purposes, sometimes bad; but whether the end is benign or evil, great leaders are those men and women who leave their personal stamp on history.

Now, the very concept of leadership implies the proposition that individuals can make a difference. This proposition has never been universally accepted. From classical times to the present day, eminent thinkers have regarded individuals as no more than the agents and pawns of larger forces, whether the gods and goddesses of the ancient world or, in the modern era, race, class, nation, the dialectic, the will of the people, the spirit of the times, history itself. Against such forces, the individual dwindles into insignificance.

So contends the thesis of historical determinism. Tolstoy's great novel *War and Peace* offers a famous statement of the case. Why, Tolstoy asked, did millions of men in the Napoleonic Wars, denying their human feelings and their common sense, move back and forth across Europe slaughtering their fellows? "The war," Tolstoy answered, "was bound to happen simply because it was bound to happen." All prior history predetermined it. As for leaders, they, Tolstoy said, "are but the labels that serve to give a name to an end and, like labels, they have the least possible connection with the event." The greater the leader, "the more conspicuous the inevitability and the predestination of every act he commits." The leader, said Tolstoy, is "the slave of history."

Determinism takes many forms. Marxism is the determinism of class. Nazism the determinism of race. But the idea of men and women as the slaves of history runs athwart the deepest human instincts. Rigid determinism abolishes the idea of human freedom—

the assumption of free choice that underlies every move we make, every word we speak, every thought we think. It abolishes the idea of human responsibility, since it is manifestly unfair to reward or punish people for actions that are by definition beyond their control. No one can live consistently by any deterministic creed. The Marxist states prove this themselves by their extreme susceptibility to the cult of leadership.

More than that, history refutes the idea that individuals make no difference. In December 1931 a British politician crossing Park Avenue in New York City between 76th and 77th Streets around 10:30 P.M. looked in the wrong direction and was knocked down by an automobile—a moment, he later recalled, of a man aghast, a world aglare: "I do not understand why I was not broken like an eggshell or squashed like a gooseberry." Fourteen months later an American politician, sitting in an open car in Miami, Florida, was fired on by an assassin; the man beside him was hit. Those who believe that individuals make no difference to history might well ponder whether the next two decades would have been the same had Mario Constasino's car killed Winston Churchill in 1931 and Giuseppe Zangara's bullet killed Franklin Roosevelt in 1933. Suppose, in addition, that Adolf Hitler had been killed in the street fighting during the Munich *Putsch* of 1923 and that Lenin had died of typhus during World War I. What would the 20th century be like now?

For better or for worse, individuals do make a difference. "The notion that a people can run itself and its affairs anonymously," wrote the philosopher William James, "is now well known to be the silliest of absurdities. Mankind does nothing save through initiatives on the part of inventors, great or small, and imitation by the rest of us—these are the sole factors in human progress. Individuals of genius show the way, and set the patterns, which common people then adopt and follow."

Leadership, James suggests, means leadership in thought as well as in action. In the long run, leaders in thought may well make the greater difference to the world. But, as Woodrow Wilson once said, "Those only are leaders of men, in the general eye, who lead in action. . . . It is at their hands that new thought gets its translation into the crude language of deeds." Leaders in thought often invent in solitude and obscurity, leaving to later generations the tasks of imitation. Leaders in action—the leaders portrayed in this series—have to be effective in their own time.

And they cannot be effective by themselves. They must act in response to the rhythms of their age. Their genius must be adapted, in a phrase of William James's, "to the receptivities of the moment." Leaders are useless without followers. "There goes the mob," said the French politician hearing a clamor in the streets. "I am their leader. I must follow them." Great leaders turn the inchoate emotions of the mob to purposes of their own. They seize on the opportunities of their time, the hopes, fears, frustrations, crises, potentialities. They succeed when events have prepared the way for them, when the community is awaiting to be aroused, when they can provide the clarifying and organizing ideas. Leadership ignites the circuit between the individual and the mass and thereby alters history.

It may alter history for better or for worse. Leaders have been responsible for the most extravagant follies and most monstrous crimes that have beset suffering humanity. They have also been vital in such gains as humanity has made in individual freedom, religious and racial tolerance, social justice, and respect for human rights.

There is no sure way to tell in advance who is going to lead for good and who for evil. But a glance at the gallery of men and women in *World Leaders—Past and Present* suggests some useful tests.

One test is this: Do leaders lead by force or by persuasion? By command or by consent? Through most of history leadership was exercised by the divine right of authority. The duty of followers was to defer and to obey. "Theirs not to reason why / Theirs but to do and die." On occasion, as with the so-called enlightened despots of the 18th century in Europe, absolutist leadership was animated by humane purposes. More often, absolutism nourished the passion for domination, land, gold, and conquest and resulted in tyranny.

The great revolution of modern times has been the revolution of equality. The idea that all people should be equal in their legal condition has undermined the old structure of authority, hierarchy, and deference. The revolution of equality has had two contrary effects on the nature of leadership. For equality, as Alexis de Tocqueville pointed out in his great study *Democracy in America,* might mean equality in servitude as well as equality in freedom.

"I know of only two methods of establishing equality in the political world," Tocqueville wrote. "Rights must be given to every citizen, or none at all to anyone . . . save one, who is the master of all." There was no middle ground "between the sovereignty of all and the absolute power of one man." In his astonishing prediction of 20th-century totalitarian dictatorship, Tocqueville explained how the revolution of equality could lead to the *"Führerprinzip"* and more terrible absolutism than the world had ever known.

But when rights are given to every citizen and the sovereignty of all is established, the problem of leadership takes a new form, becomes more exacting than ever before. It is easy to issue commands and enforce them by the rope and the stake, the concentration camp and the *gulag.* It is much harder to use argument and achievement to overcome opposition and win consent. The Founding Fathers of the United States understood the difficulty. They believed that history had given them the opportunity to decide, as Alexander Hamilton wrote in the first Federalist Paper, whether men are indeed capable of basing government on "reflection and choice, or whether they are forever destined to depend . . . on accident and force."

Government by reflection and choice called for a new style of leadership and a new quality of followership. It required leaders to be responsive to popular concerns, and it required followers to be active and informed participants in the process. Democracy does not eliminate emotion from politics; sometimes it fosters demagoguery; but it is confident that, as the greatest of democratic leaders put it, you cannot fool all of the people all of the time. It measures leadership by results and retires those who overreach or falter or fail.

It is true that in the long run despots are measured by results too. But they can postpone the day of judgment, sometimes indefinitely, and in the meantime they can do infinite harm. It is also true that democracy is no guarantee of virtue and intelligence in government, for the voice of the people is not necessarily the voice of God. But democracy, by assuring the right of opposition, offers built-in resistance to the evils inherent in absolutism. As the theologian Reinhold Niebuhr summed it up, "Man's capacity for justice makes democracy possible, but man's inclination to injustice makes democracy necessary."

A second test for leadership is the end for which power is sought. When leaders have as their goal the supremacy of a master race or the promotion of totalitarian revolution or the acquisition and exploitation of colonies or the protection of greed and privilege or the preservation of personal power, it is likely that their leadership will do little to advance the cause of humanity. When their goal is the abolition of slavery, the liberation of women, the enlargement of opportunity for the poor and powerless, the extension of equal rights to racial minorities, the defense of the freedoms of expression and opposition, it is likely that their leadership will increase the sum of human liberty and welfare.

Leaders have done great harm to the world. They have also conferred great benefits. You will find both sorts in this series. Even "good" leaders must be regarded with a certain wariness. Leaders are not demigods; they put on their trousers one leg after another just like ordinary mortals. No leader is infallible, and every leader needs to be reminded of this at regular intervals. Irreverence irritates leaders but is their salvation. Unquestioning submission corrupts leaders and demeans followers. Making a cult of a leader is always a mistake. Fortunately hero worship generates its own antidote. "Every hero," said Emerson, "becomes a bore at last."

The signal benefit the great leaders confer is to embolden the rest of us to live according to our own best selves, to be active, insistent, and resolute in affirming our own sense of things. For great leaders attest to the reality of human freedom against the supposed inevitabilities of history. And they attest to the wisdom and power that may lie within the most unlikely of us, which is why Abraham Lincoln remains the supreme example of great leadership. A great leader, said Emerson, exhibits new possibilities to all humanity. "We feed on genius. . . . Great men exist that there may be greater men."

Great leaders, in short, justify themselves by emancipating and empowering their followers. So humanity struggles to master its destiny, remembering with Alexis de Tocqueville: "It is true that around every man a fatal circle is traced beyond which he cannot pass; but within the wide verge of that circle he is powerful and free; as it is with man, so with communities."

1

The Martyr

The lights burned past midnight and on into the early hours of August 21, 1983, at the Aquino home on the corner of Commonwealth Avenue and Mt. Alvernia Road in Newton, Massachusetts. The residents of the three-story brick house were restless. Maria Elena, the oldest Aquino daughter, tried to distract herself by reading about baseball. Meanwhile, her mother, Corazon, was trying desperately to sleep as her youngest daughter, Kristina, lay beside her in bed. But for the Aquinos there was no peace. Maria Elena recalled, "I could feel my heart beating faster and faster." At 1:10 A.M. her mother got up. "I've been trying to sleep for so long," Corazon said wearily to Maria Elena, "I don't know if I was able to sleep at all." She then headed back to bed.

When the telephone rang less than an hour later, Maria Elena picked up the receiver to hear the voice of a family friend asking if the Aquinos had heard any news from the Philippines. Corazon had talked with her husband, Benigno, in Taiwan about six hours earlier, but since then the family had heard nothing. He would be in Manila, the capital of the Philippines, by now.

The Filipino is worth dying for.
—BENIGNO AQUINO

Former Philippine senator Benigno S. Aquino, Jr., was an outspoken opponent of the dictatorial regime of Ferdinand Marcos. In August 1983, having lived in exile in the United States for three years, Aquino made the fateful decision to return to his country in an attempt to persuade Marcos to relinquish power.

At 2:30 A.M. the telephone rang again. Corazon arose to see who was calling, but Maria Elena answered first. It was a reporter from New York City, who spoke of conflicting news stories and wanted verification from the family. "What is it?" Corazon asked as her daughter put down the telephone. Visibly shaken, Maria Elena said, "The man said somebody was shot."

Just eight days before, in the early hours of August 13, Corazon Aquino had gone through another sleepness night. For weeks she had been uneasy over the trip Benigno was going to take. In a few hours, "Ninoy," as his family and friends called him, would leave her, the children, and the comfortable Georgian-style home they had shared for three years in exile to embark on a dramatic return to their island country in the Pacific, the Philippines. There he would confront his enemies, President Ferdinand E. Marcos and the formidable first lady, Imelda.

With his wife, Corazon, and daughter Maria Elena, Benigno Aquino reads cards from well-wishers after undergoing heart surgery in Texas. During his seven-year imprisonment in the Philippines Aquino developed a heart ailment, and in 1980, under pressure from human-rights groups, Marcos released him.

Members of the New People's Army prepare for an attack. Because Marcos's dictatorship permitted no legal political freedom, many Filipinos felt their only recourse was to join the radical communist rebels, whose goal was to take over the government by revolution.

Powerful as the Marcoses were, they had always feared Benigno Aquino's political savvy and widespread popularity among the Filipinos. In 1972 Aquino had been the man everyone expected to see elected the next president of the Philippines. Those expectations ended in September of that year when Ferdinand Marcos scrapped the country's democratic institutions and took on dictatorial powers. He immediately threw Benigno Aquino, his most potent rival, into prison. For seven years and seven months, Marcos sealed Aquino off from his political supporters and effectively prevented him from publicly criticizing the regime. Several times during those years, Benigno came close to dying from a heart attack and the effects of a hunger strike he went on to protest his imprisonment. Marcos flashed before Aquino the constant threat of execution on trumped-up charges of murder and treason. Thus, on that restive summer night before Ninoy's departure, the thought of what might befall him as he once more challenged the Marcoses worried Corazon considerably. "Let's not talk about it," Ninoy said. "I told you long ago this is what we have to do."

Philippine senator Salvador Laurel (right) talks with Benigno Aquino in San Francisco, 1980. Laurel was a long-time friend of Aquino who remained in the Philippines to coordinate the opposition until Aquino's return.

Benigno Aquino's concern over his country's future had grown ever since Marcos, bowing to pressure from international human rights groups, had allowed him to leave the Philippines in 1980 for heart surgery in the United States. Since then, the Aquinos had lived comfortably in the Boston suburbs. The 50-year-old politician, supported by friends and his wife's wealthy family in the Philippines, lectured at the Massachusetts Institute of Technology and Harvard University. His spirits were buoyed by a constant flow of Filipino opponents of Marcos visiting the United States, but Ninoy Aquino remained preoccupied with his homeland and its problems, which seemed to worsen every year.

Since imposing martial law in 1972, Ferdinand Marcos had so monopolized wealth and power in the Philippines that Benigno believed it would lead to the country's undoing. The ranks of communist rebels in the countryside were swollen with starving peasants and disenchanted students fleeing from the bully-boy tactics of the government soldiers. Indeed, most Filipinos saw the armed forces merely as the corrupt private army of the Marcos family.

The regime tolerated very little criticism. The government handed over control of all major newspapers and television and radio stations to cronies of the president's family. Meanwhile, hundreds of Filipinos, imprisoned without trial and often tortured because of their opposition to Marcos, languished in military detention camps. Others who opposed the regime simply disappeared. Some bodies washed up on river banks or were found in forest graves; some were never recovered. Honest businessmen were exasperated because the government had turned over much of the country's largest corporations and industries to Ferdinand and Imelda's friends, who proceeded to grossly mismanage the resources that powered the national economy.

Marcos had clung so tightly to the presidency for almost two decades that he was no longer willing to leave office, nor could he bring himself to name a successor. His free-spending, jet-setting wife appeared to be scheming to start an unprecedented dynastic presidency should her husband suddenly die, intending to install herself as the next ruler of the 55 million Filipinos spread throughout the more than 7,100 islands of the archipelago. Benigno Aquino knew that Imelda Marcos could succeed with help from her allies in the military. He also knew that the military would soon dispose of her and rule on its own. These acts would only increase the already grave dissatisfaction among Filipinos and lead to massive public disorder in the cities and the countryside. If the people were caught between the twin evils of an imperious, uncaring government and the revolutionary tactics of the communists, Benigno feared that they would choose to support the violent guerrilla war the rebels were waging in the jungles, and a bloody civil war would erupt. He was afraid that this unpleasant scenario would come true all too soon, because everyone believed that Ferdinand Marcos was already dying.

Corazon Aquino was well aware of her husband's thoughts. Though she rarely spoke to neighbors or her husband's many guests — indeed, most visitors

My heart and mind and my soul—yes, every part of my being is against any form of dictatorship.
—BENIGNO AQUINO

Philippine first lady Imelda Marcos dances with American actor George Hamilton in January 1983. Mrs. Marcos visited Benigno Aquino in the United States to warn him of threats against his life if he returned to the Philippines.

saw her only when she served coffee or prepared gourmet meals — "Cory" Aquino listened carefully to all the political theorizing that went on in her home. When everyone was gone, she would give her husband her opinions, counseling him for or against the various views that cropped up during the discussions. He rarely made an important political decision without first sounding out his wife. Thus, Corazon knew how her husband hoped to prevent the catastrophe everyone envisioned for the Philippines.

Benigno Aquino believed that only Ferdinand Marcos was in a position to save the country. By voluntarily relinquishing his dictatorship, Marcos could restore democracy and thus save the Philippines from the terrible fate that seemed to await it. The action would serve Marcos well. Aquino recalled that Marcos once phoned him in prison to say, "In a way, I envy you. You have earned your presence in history. I'm still fighting for mine." Marcos could go down in history not as a power-hungry tyrant but as a benevolent ruler who selflessly abdicated total power for the sake of his country. Benigno believed that if this line of reasoning was presented to Marcos, it would be an argument that the pragmatic president would relish. It would also provide a graceful way for Marcos to give up full responsibility for the country's problems. But Benigno also knew that the people around the president, who profited from being close to the center of power, were unlikely to advise him to give up the dictatorship. Thus, before Marcos died, before Imelda and the military attempted to rule in his place, before the communist rebellion in the countryside turned into a full-scale revolution, the situation required the dramatic return of a man who would have no reason to wish Marcos well but who would selflessly choose to do so. It required the return of Benigno Aquino.

In Aquino's vision, he and Marcos would meet and dismiss their enmity. Then, convinced by Aquino of the wisdom of restoring democracy peacefully, Marcos would hold fair elections, allow the opposition, led by Aquino, to share power and responsibility for the country's future, and thus avert disaster for the nation. By returning home while

A view of the Philippine countryside. The Philippines enjoys a tropical climate, and the terrain varies from sandy beaches to inland rain forests and mountainous regions.

still under the death sentence originally imposed in 1977 and reaffirmed by Marcos in July 1983, Benigno hoped to prove to Marcos that he was sincere about cooperating with him. In a speech he planned to deliver upon his return, Benigno wrote, "I could have opted to seek political asylum in America, but I feel it is my duty, as it is the duty of every Filipino, to suffer with his people especially in time of crisis." He hoped to touch Marcos, to move him emotionally to seek a peaceful solution to the approaching turmoil. Aquino hoped that his sincerity would convert Marcos to the cause of democracy.

Corazon Aquino did not share her husband's assessment of Marcos. "I told Ninoy that Marcos would not listen to him," she later wrote in a magazine article, adding "that the man is completely calloused." Ninoy only said, "I will never forgive myself if I did not at least try." Even though the three years spent in Massachusetts had been, as Corazon later said, "the happiest of their lives together," Benigno could not be dissuaded from leaving the United States for home.

With the help of his family, Benigno Aquino packs for his return to the Philippines in August 1983. Aquino was aware of the danger he faced, but he feared that if he did not try to provide an alternative to Marcos, his country would descend into a bloody civil war.

Yet for all his bravery, Benigno was nervous on that last night in Massachusetts. Since May, letters and emissaries from the Marcoses had been warning him not to return. Three months earlier Imelda Marcos herself had met with Benigno in New York City to tell him that Philippine intelligence agents had detected an assassination plot against him and that the government could not guarantee his safety. Imelda offered to help establish Aquino in some business or other, as long as he stayed in the United States. Otherwise, Imelda hinted, the Marcoses might not be able to control what happened to him. As insurance, Imelda held Benigno's passport; if he wanted to return to the Philippines he had to apply for it at a government office. It was unlikely that she would allow her officials to release it.

Benigno Aquino decided that Imelda's implied threat was merely a ploy to keep him separated from his followers in the Philippines and to prevent him from trying to reach a peaceful political settlement with the regime. He ignored her and prepared for his return. He had planned to arrive in Manila on August 7, but Marcos's defense minister, Juan Ponce Enrile, informed him of another plot against his life and encouraged him to wait a month. Benigno, fearful that the government was trying to cheat him out of time to prepare for the upcoming legislative elections, postponed his arrival in Manila by only two weeks.

Thus, the early hours of August 13, 1983, passed restlessly for the Aquinos in Newton. In the morning, Benigno and Corazon, accompanied by their five children — Maria Elena, Aurora, Benigno III, Victoria, and Kristina — attended mass at St. Ignatius Roman Catholic Church. The intensely religious family prayed hard for his safety. "Although we tried to hide our apprehension," Corazon later wrote, "Ninoy and I could feel each other's sadness." There were no tears; it was not her style.

Benigno Aquino spent a week slipping away from Marcos agents on his trail, hopping from Los Angeles to Singapore to Malaysia, back to Singapore and finally to Taipei, the capital of Taiwan. He awoke

> *A time comes in a man's life when he must prefer a meaningful death to a meaningless life. I would rather die on my feet with honor, than live on bended knees in shame.*
> —BENIGNO AQUINO
> from speech at his trial

Benigno Aquino takes a moment to pray before his plane lands at Manila, the Philippine capital. Aquino had prepared a speech to deliver to his supporters waiting at the airport, but he had barely stepped off the plane before he was assassinated.

at his hotel in Tapei at 5:00 A.M. on a hot and humid August 21, ready at last to return to Manila. He hoped to catch the Philippine authorities unawares.

They knew of his plan to return, but if they discovered the airline and flight he was on, the Philippine air force could turn the plane away before it landed. Marcos's officials could also whisk him away immediately upon his arrival, thus depriving him of a flashy appearance at the airport for the hundreds of followers who had gathered to welcome him. But Benigno believed he had eluded the Filipino agents. Despite his familiar face, no one at the various airports he had traveled through seemed to recognize him. No one questioned the forged passport he carried under the ironic alias "Marcial Bonifacio," named for the martial law regime and for Fort Bonifacio, one of the prisons he had been held in.

It was an uncomfortable morning in Taipei's ornate Grand Hotel. The previous night Benigno had talked brashly with the reporters who had found him. Many asked about the rumored assassination plot. "Assassination is part of public service," Benigno said. "If my fate is to die by an assassin's bullet so be it. But I cannot be petrified by inaction or fear of assassination and therefore stay in a corner." He expected Marcos to do no more than put him under house arrest. For publicity's sake, he displayed the bulletproof vest he planned to wear at the airport in Manila. "But if they hit me in the head," he said almost jokingly, "I'm a goner."

It was at that meeting with reporters that one correspondent mentioned the warning made by the Philippine armed forces chief of staff, General Fabian C. Ver, that Benigno Aquino might be murdered by unknown — perhaps communist — assailants at the airport. Benigno was genuinely shocked and shortly thereafter explained his apprehension about Ver to his traveling companion, his American brother-in-law, Ken Kashiwahara, a correspondent for ABC News. Ver was not known for taking personal initiatives. He was so loyal to Marcos that if the president "asked him to jump from a building, [Ver] would salute and ask, 'From what floor, sir?' " Was this warning a bluff to scare Benigno off? Or had something more sinister been planned?

On the morning of August 21, after reciting his prayers, Benigno called his wife. As was her custom, Corazon read random passages from the Bible to him, hoping to find spiritual guidance. On the phone with his wife and children, Benigno cried, and after he hung up, he wrote letters to each of them.

At 9:30 A.M. Aquino left the Grand Hotel. With his brother-in-law, Benigno reminisced about Cory and the happy life they had led in Boston during the last three years. He recalled the seven years he had spent in prison and how Cory, alone, had held the family together as friends and supporters, cowed by the political strength of the Marcos regime, faded away. "One regret I have," he said, "is that Cory has had to suffer so much."

Benigno's flight to Manila on China Airlines left Taipei at 11:15 A.M. He was in an exuberant mood on the airplane and made a display of putting on his bulletproof vest in front of reporters who had joined him. The presence of so many foreign journalists was reassuring. Benigno felt that Marcos would not try anything so blatantly stupid as an assassination while dozens of reporters were recording his opponent's return. Some Filipinos on the plane recognized Aquino and asked for his autograph. About two hours later, the plane arrived at Manila International Airport.

As soon as the engines of the Boeing 767 shut down, the airport jetway snaked its arm onto the plane's front exit and three soldiers boarded. It was 1:10 A.M.; halfway around the world, in Massachusetts, Corazon Aquino had just left her bed, unable to sleep.

"Noy," Kashiwahara said, "They're coming to get you." The first soldier almost passed Benigno by, but the soldier in dark glasses behind him recognized the exile. The moment the second soldier noticed the cameras of Japanese and American television journalists trained on him, he raised a hand to his face. The third soldier also shielded his face from the TV cameras, but he still had the presence of mind to shake Aquino's hand. Benigno smiled. The second soldier put his arm behind Benigno and felt the bulletproof vest, and the two exchanged words.

Benigno rose from his seat. One soldier held his bag, the other grabbed him tightly by the arm. They moved down the aisle. "I'm coming with him," said Kashiwahara suddenly, "I'm his brother-in-law." The soldier in the dark glasses snapped, "You just take your seat." Benigno was no longer smiling.

At Manila Airport, Benigno Aquino (in white) lies dead from a bullet to the head while officials secure the area. To Aquino's left is Rolando Galman, the alleged assassin, who was killed by airport security men.

Several plainclothes government security agents were at the plane's exit by the time Aquino reached the jetway tunnel leading into the airport terminal. Suddenly, a side door on the jetway was opened onto a stairway descending to the airport's tarmac. The soldiers swung Benigno toward this exit, while the plainclothesmen stopped reporters from following. The agents' hands blocked the lenses of television cameras and their bodies sealed off the exit immediately after Aquino began making his way down the steps. Less than ten seconds later, a gunshot rang out.

"The man said somebody was shot." Corazon Aquino knew from her daughter's expression that she was talking about Ninoy. "I tried to believe it was a false report," she recalled three years later. As more rumors reached her, she hoped the wound was not fatal. But a friend of her husband's in the Japanese government called and confirmed his death. The reports spoke of blood spouting from the back of Aquino's head.

"The children and I cried when I told them the bad news," Corazon said. "After a few minutes, we all knelt down to pray the Rosary and ask the Blessed Mother for help."

Together, Benigno and Corazon Aquino take in the view from their San Francisco apartment, 1980. Benigno's death was the beginning of Corazon's political life, as the grieving widow struggled to draw some meaning from her loss.

2

The Widow

Unaware of the carnage on the tarmac, 20,000 well-wishers waited for Benigno Aquino to emerge from the airport terminal. They had originally planned to be at the plane to greet him but the government refused them permission to enter the building. Instead, they waited outside, waving banners for their returning hero: *We Love You Ninoy* and *Ninoy, You Are Not Alone!* Hundreds, perhaps thousands, of yellow ribbons, symbols of the public solidarity, decked the city's telephone poles, walls, and trees. Although the Marcos regime had banned antigovernment slogans, there was no rule against ribbons, and Manila was festooned with a silent rebellion of yellow, a celebration of the return of Benigno Aquino, Ferdinand Marcos's greatest foe.

As Benigno's 75-year-old mother, Aurora Aquino, presided over the gathering, his childhood friend and classmate Salvador Laurel tried to get word of his arrival. Soon enough, however, passengers from the fatal flight began trickling out of the terminal.

> *Cory Aquino became a real Cory Aquino only when Ninoy died. Everybody had to notice her, because Ninoy was gone.*
> —TESSIE ORETA
> Benigno Aquino's sister

Corazon Cojuangco as she appeared in her college yearbook. She was educated in Catholic schools in the United States. During her college years she began a correspondence with Benigno Aquino, and in 1954, a year after her return to the Philippines, she married the dashing politician.

Word of "Ninoy's" return to the Philippines had spread, and more than 20,000 supporters were waiting at Manila Airport to greet him. Barred from entering the terminal, they waited outside with banners and yellow ribbons to show their solidarity.

Returning to the waiting crowds, Laurel picked up a bullhorn. "I have sad news for you," he said, his face etched with the sharp lines of shock. "Ninoy, our beloved, is back, but you might not be able to see him. Eyewitnesses say he has been shot!" Suddenly hushed, the crowd drifted away, confused and afraid. Benigno's sister wept. His mother stood unsmiling, betraying no emotion.

In Massachusetts, Corazon Aquino prepared for her trip home. It would be a difficult departure. She had been so happy in Newton. She had enjoyed relaxing in front of the television and dabbling in the kitchen, cooking up everything from exotic Philippine sweets to crisp Peking duck. Benigno had been happy too, staying up at night playing mah-jongg and discussing politics with his friends, raising dogs, vacationing in Cape Cod with his children — the kinds of things the family had missed while he was in Marcos's prison.

Corazon gathered together the mementos of her life with Ninoy: wedding pictures, knickknacks, dresses he had bought for her, and a poem he had written about her almost 10 years earlier. In it, he described her as "unruffled by trouble, undeterred by the load." She could do with that strength now. She talked to a physician about tranquilizers but chose not to take any. Instead, she stoically faced reporters, giving them short, brave answers. When they asked her to speak of her sorrow, she said, "Ninoy often said all the years after he went on a hunger strike in 1975 were bonus years and we should just be grateful we had them." Was she afraid to return home? "I have no hesitation whatsoever." She did not weep in public. Only once, after friends of her husband said they planned to transform her Newton home into a memorial to Ninoy, did she cry in front of visitors. It would be hard adjusting to life without him.

Corazon Cojuangco married Benigno Servillano Aquino, Jr., on October 11, 1954. He was a brilliant young journalist, law student, and budding politician, a member of the politically prominent Aquino family of Tarlac province in central Luzon. She was the shy, slender daughter of Jose and Demetria Cojuangco, rich sugar-plantation owners from the same province.

In 1933 Senator Benigno Aquino, Sr., (standing, third from right) poses with the group of U.S. congressmen and Filipino officials who fought for Philippine independence from the United States. The Aquino family had a long tradition of political activism.

Both families were among the most prominent in the country. Benigno Aquino was descended from a Filipino general in the wars of independence against Spain and later against the Americans, who won the islands in the Spanish-American War of 1898. Even after those wars, the Aquinos, like most upper- and middle-class families of the Spanish period, kept their high social standing, if not their wealth. Benigno's father was a leading politician and served as majority floor leader of the Philippine Congress, which was set up by American colonizers in the 1920s and 1930s. The voice of Benigno Aquino, Sr., who was widely respected, was among the loudest of those calling for Philippine independence from the United States. His reputation was sullied by his decision to work with the Japanese, who occupied the Philippines during World War II. After the war, the Senior Aquino's great popularity saved him from execution as a wartime collaborator.

Philippine president Ramon Magsaysay poses with his family in 1955. Benigno Aquino learned the political ropes while working for Magsaysay as a press relations officer and negotiator with the peasant rebels in the countryside.

The founder of the Cojuangco family was an immigrant from China. In 1861, 13-year-old Co Guioc Huang left the turmoil of the Chinese Empire to make a new life for himself in the nearby Spanish-ruled islands of the Philippines. Taking a job as a carpenter and woodworker, Co worked on the re-modeling of Malacañang Palace, which became the sumptuous home of the Spanish governor generals, American colonial rulers, and Philippine presidents. After saving up enough money, Co Guioc Huang started his own business and was granted the Hispanicized name Jose Cojuangco. In 1896, considerably wealthier, Jose Cojuangco moved to Tarlac province. The Cojuangco family came to own a vast amount of property in central Luzon on which they established rice and sugar plantations. Jose Cojuangco's descendants continued to use Tarlac as a political and economic power base.

Due to the wealth and status of her family, Maria Corazon Cojuangco, born on January 25, 1933, enjoyed a privileged childhood. The Cojuangcos and Aquinos traveled in the same social circles; as a result, Corazon and Benigno knew each other as children. They ran across each other at parties, including a birthday celebration in 1941 at the

Schoolgirls in Quezon City waiting for the funeral procession of Benigno Aquino display banners with the words, "Ninoy, you are not alone." Corazon Aquino was stunned by the massive outpouring of grief and support for her late husband.

Aquino home that Corazon remembers particularly well. It was the first time she clearly distinguished Ninoy from the other children at the huge socials she and her family attended. She recalled that it was not love at first sight. In fact, she was peeved over the precocious Ninoy's bratty behavior and his boast that, even though they were the same age, he was a year ahead of her in school. As a teenager, Corazon saw less of Benigno; most of the time she was in the United States, studying at exclusive convent schools. Eventually she enrolled at the College of Mount St. Vincent, a Roman Catholic institution in New York City.

For his part, Benigno Aquino had begun a successful career as a journalist, establishing his reputation as a 17-year-old Korean War correspondent during the 1950s. As something of a celebrity bachelor, the dashing Benigno dated beauty queens and high society ladies. Among his many dates was the stunning Imelda Romualdez, the future wife of Ferdinand Marcos, who at the time was trying to rise from her childhood of genteel poverty by way of a minor beauty title. At Manila's glittering social functions, Benigno often joked that Imelda was "too tall for me" and refused to dance with her. But they saw much of each other in 1953 and considered each other good friends. Later, however, after they had become political enemies, Imelda would viciously hint that Benigno had chosen money over beauty and had "abandoned" her for the wealthy heiress Corazon Cojuangco.

One summer, while Benigno was basking in his fame and scooping stories for the newspaper he worked for, he again met Corazon Cojuangco, who was back in Manila during a break from her mathematics and French studies at the College of Mount St. Vincent. By now, Benigno no longer seemed to irritate her. She felt he was "the most articulate guy I had met. If he was not mature in years, in outlook he was." During her last year at Mount St. Vincent, they corresponded regularly. The notes soon became love letters, which she proudly describes as "not mushy."

When Corazon returned to the Philippines in 1953 to study law, Benigno was already asking to marry her. "I thought it best for us to wait," she recalled. Patiently, Benigno took Corazon out on dates, strictly chaperoned by one of her sisters. Her parents did not disapprove of Benigno; he would make an excellent son-in-law. He was from a family that, although not as rich as the Cojuangcos, was still extremely influential in Philippine politics. Benigno was also a star reporter and seemed to be on the verge of a successful political career. However, the Cojuangcos wanted to be convinced of his devotion to their daughter.

On one occasion, Benigno's white Buick was struck by another car with such force that Corazon and one of her sisters were thrown out onto the highway. Benigno escaped unhurt but the Cojuangco sisters were bruised and sore. Corazon even had to stay overnight at a hospital. Unfortunately, her parents expected her the next night at the northern resort town of Baguio for a formal ball. When Corazon dutifully made the trip to Baguio, Benigno followed. Embarrassed by the accident and hoping to prove the seriousness of his intentions, Benigno quickly asked the elder Cojuangcos for their daughter's hand in marriage. That was the only way, he later joked, that he would get her back into his car. He would always tell Corazon that "you fell from that car on purpose to force me to marry you."

A group of young men express their outrage at the assassination of Benigno Aquino. Antigovernment demonstrations were illegal under Marcos, but the dictator could not suppress the hundreds of thousands of Filipinos who displayed their anger and grief on this occasion.

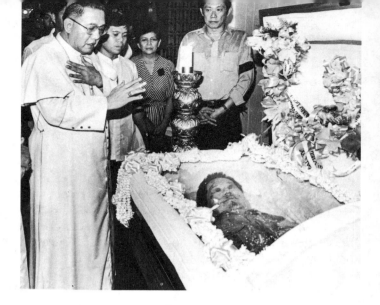

Jaime Cardinal Sin offers prayers for Benigno Aquino. Aquino's mother had refused to let the undertakers retouch her son's wounds so that the Filipino people could see the violence done to their beloved Benigno.

The wedding was celebrated in Pasay City, a suburb of Manila. The bride wore a gown of white tulle and silk in the style of a Spanish *terno*, an elegant design that showed off Cory's long neck and gently sloping shoulders. The groom wore the traditional loose Filipino shirt called the *barong*. The chief sponsor at the wedding was Philippine president Ramon Magsaysay, whom Benigno had served as a negotiator between the government and communist rebel troops in the countryside. The best man at the ceremony was Salvador Laurel, Benigno's classmate and friend.

After a four-month honeymoon in the United States, Corazon Aquino settled down to be the wife of the latest superstar in Philippine politics. In quick succession, Benigno was elected the youngest mayor, the youngest governor, and the youngest senator in the country's history. In 1972 he seemed on the verge of becoming the youngest president of the Philippines. While Benigno was making his political mark, Corazon remained in the background with their children. She had left law school to marry Benigno and was, in a way, glad to have given up an active public life for the life of a housewife and mother. Though the Cojuangcos were involved in politics, Corazon preferred religion and meditation to politics. She never liked the grandstanding and self-serving machinations of Filipino politicos. She was never comfortable with the campaign forays her husband undertook into villages that had no toilets or electricity. She preferred escaping from the turmoil of Philippine politics into the comforts of home and family. From them she drew her security as Benigno reached for worldly power.

Suddenly, as Corazon wrote, "Ninoy's luck ran out." In September 1972 President Marcos, in order to prolong his term of office, declared martial law. At that moment, her husband's political ascendance came to an abrupt halt. Corazon thought she might lose him to prison — or worse. Benigno was tried on ludicrous charges of murder, subversion, and illegal possession of weapons and was sentenced to seven years in prison. Corazon has called those years "the most difficult period of our marriage." But in a strange way, it brought them closer than they had ever been before. Her irrepressible husband could not give up politics even within the confines of his cell. During her visits, she would bring him news of the outside world and sneak out his messages to the small band of Filipinos still loyal to him. She became his eyes and ears and eventually his mouthpiece. In the privacy of her visits to Ninoy in jail, they discovered the strength of their marriage.

In 1980 she seemed to have won him back when he was allowed to fly to the United States for medical help after he suffered his heart attack. In Boston she wrote a haiku celebrating the joy of reunion with her husband:

> The worst of my life
> is over, I hope.
> And may the best
> please come soon.

Much later, however, she would say, "I remember when I read it to Ninoy, he said, 'I don't think you have experienced the worst yet. There is so much we have to do.' " In August 1983 he left for Manila, and she lost him forever. As Corazon prepared for the trip to Manila to bury her husband, she thought that once the funeral was over she would be alone with her family and her memories. After all, she thought, what would anyone want to do with the widow of a dead politician?

A huge crowd fills the street outside Santo Domingo church in Quezon City to view Benigno Aquino's coffin on its way to the cemetery. Corazon, aware of the people's volatile mood, had ordered that the funeral procession avoid Malacañang Palace to avert any possible violence.

As for the Filipinos, she had long ago come to a conclusion that her husband never accepted: "Filipinos are cowards." With Benigno gone, they would cower before Marcos's political might. After Marcos jailed her husband in 1972, people who once had flocked to Benigno, in hopes of advancing their own careers when he became president, quickly learned to avoid her. Former friends crossed the street to keep from associating with the wife of the chief enemy of the regime. Corazon was convinced that this time it would be no different; the Filipinos were still cowards.

Over the phone, she told her relatives that she wanted Ninoy's wake to be held at the compact but

comfortable bungalow they had shared on Times
Street, in Quezon City on the outskirts of Manila.
She did not think they needed much room for visitors. "After all we had gone through from 1972 to
1983," she said, "I felt we really had very few
friends." Before she left the United States, however,
Corazon received a surprising call from her sister,
asking permission to move Ninoy to a bigger house.
Corazon was shocked to learn that mourners were
dropping by the Aquino house on Times Street at
the rate of 40 or 50 a minute.

In the beginning, there had been no crowds because the people were too afraid. Manila's streets
were wild with rumor and panic, and, as the gov-

ernment clamped down on information about the assassination, Filipinos passed off speculation as fact. Reports circulated that Marcos had died and that the generals and Imelda had taken over. Housewives, afraid that street fighting would cut off their food supplies, ransacked the supermarket shelves. The very night of Benigno's death, a major blackout plunged metropolitan Manila and its 8 million inhabitants, as well as most of the huge island of Luzon, into darkness. People thought there had been a military coup. No one knew what was going on. Marcos himself was nowhere in sight. Only 30 hours after Benigno's death did the president finally come on TV to accuse the communists of killing his rival. Few Filipinos believed him.

Slowly, people started trickling into the Aquino home. None of the larger papers said much about the assassination. Only the smaller opposition magazines mentioned it in detail. Television barely covered the event, and only Radio Veritas, the station of the Roman Catholic church, reported on the shooting in full. But people somehow found out that Ninoy's body was at his home in Quezon City. In a dramatic gesture, Ninoy's mother had ordered that her son's casket be left open so that his body could be shown to the public in its bloodied clothes, the wounds unretouched. She wanted the Filipinos to see her son as he had fallen.

As the days went on, hundreds of Filipinos, from wealthy aristocratic matrons to dusty street urchins, were lining up to honor Ninoy. Taxi drivers whose busy schedules gave them no time to visit during the day went in the middle of the night. The poorly dressed women with large reed baskets who worked as fish vendors walked in at sunrise before making their way to the market. They all came to show the Aquino family that they cared. Vicente Paterno, a member of Marcos's party at the time, said that people were mourning Ninoy in the streets. He overheard one old woman say, "They are so cruel. He was returning to his country; they did not even let him step on the soil of his native land." Feelings of disgust and bitterness welled up. The signs that were meant to greet him at the airport were displayed again: *Ninoy, You Are Not Alone.* Indeed, he was not. Students, businessmen, actors, truckdrivers, the humble and the proud, all came to see Ninoy.

Filipinos, said Paterno, were furious at what seemed to be a media cover-up. "They were being denied the news, so they went to see for themselves. They felt real outrage, indignation, and anger." People brought tiny bits of tribute: strings of the sweet-smelling *sampaguita*, a jasmine commonly sold on the streets of Manila, and blooms of the rose-colored hibiscus Filipinos call the *gumamela*. Some parents brought their children to see history in the making. Others brought only themselves and their tears.

These were the people Corazon Aquino met when she reached Manila a few days later. Dressed in black, she had at first requested to be alone with her husband, but when she noticed the huge crowds gathered outside her Times Street home, she thought better of it. She later said, "I did not feel it was right that they should be waiting so long."

She was still surprised that so many people had come out for Ninoy. "It was really amazing," she related in the book *People Power.* "Knowing the strict censorship of the media, I was afraid that the people did not even know that Ninoy had been assassinated." Never before in her country's history had there been such public mourning. Corazon, tired and confused, did not know what to make of the phenomenon.

The crowds, however, quickly took away an image that would be deeply etched in their consciousness: Corazon Aquino calmly gazing at her husband, making the sign of the cross and praying. She shed no tears and kept a steely, stoic determination on her face. Later, they heard that she had bent low to whisper to Ninoy that she would carry on the work he had left unfinished.

When Ninoy's body was brought to his native province of Tarlac, the crowds were almost wild with grief. "The people were all over the hearse," Corazon recalled. "It looked like a mob. I was not prepared for that." She added, "Widows don't normally go through this." Taking Ninoy from Tarlac back to Manila for burial, however, Cory was touched by the gentleness and sympathy of the crowds. The thousands that lined the highway offered her soft drinks and food. She was grateful for their care, because she was exhausted. The 24-hour flight from the United States and the many funerary ceremonies were taking their toll. Still, in the midst of the preparations for Ninoy's burial, she managed to be strong. She recalled, "The crowds had become a strange sort of comfort. I kept thinking, 'Ninoy is really so happy, now that people really care.' I think I would have collapsed if it was just my family and I who had to take care of [mourning and arranging for Ninoy's burial]."

On August 31, Jaime Cardinal Sin, spiritual leader of all Roman Catholics in the Philippines, said a funeral mass for Benigno Aquino at the imposing Santo Domingo church in Quezon City. Crowds gathered on the streets, lining the route between the church and Manila Memorial Park, where Benigno would be interred. More than 2 million people ignored the rain to pack the city's streets. The government-controlled press cast virtually a blind eye to the funeral. In fact, one pro-Marcos paper ignored the millions of people who stood eight hours to catch a glimpse of the funeral procession. Instead, it headlined a tree struck by lightning.

On the streets, however, Filipinos made sure they were part of the event. Thousands carried yellow banners and shouted Ninoy's name. Paterno explained, "It was an act of penitence. They were trying to show their contrition for having allowed such a thing to happen." Indeed, many Filipinos felt ashamed at having allowed a dictator such as Marcos to have had his way for so many years. They despised what they felt to be their own cowardice. Paterno added, "They were chanting and applauding not because it was a funeral procession, but because it was a hero's procession. Ninoy is a hero in the most accepted Filipino sense, because he achieved by his death an awakening of the Filipino conscience."

Although grateful for the outpouring of affection, Corazon was well aware of the potential for an outbreak of violence. If she had allowed the procession to pass Malacañang, the presidential palace, the millions would have turned against Marcos in anger. She wisely asked them to avoid that route. Emmanuel Pelaez, who would eventually become her ambassador to the United States, later said that if she had only given the word, the Marcoses would have been chased out of the country immediately. Corazon, however, did not tap the potential for vengeance.

During the funeral, Corazon recalled the conversation she had had with her husband about the character of their countrymen. "Filipinos are cowards," she had said. "No," Ninoy had replied, "All they need is a leader."

3

The Enemy

The Philippines, however, did have a leader. And if he was no longer a truly inspiring one, he was still a proud and autocratic ruler who exercised near absolute power. When he became president of the Republic of the Philippines in November 1965, Ferdinand Edralin Marcos held the elements of historical greatness in his grasp. The usually disorderly and fractious Filipinos admired him for his charisma and for his immense intellectual gifts. He offered them a sense of national unity with his vision of a homegrown style of democracy. Furthermore, his shrewd tactics and determination to get things done his way impressed both his people and his chief ally, the United States. Through guile and bravado he instilled in them the perception that he could not be replaced. But as Marcos clung to power through the years, he grew increasingly corrupt. In the end, he became the master of the half-truth and the blatant lie, holding on to the presidency by fooling his countrymen, as well as the United States, with falsehoods and wild promises.

What do we do if our leader dies? I guess President Marcos will have to run things by himself.
—Popular joke about Imelda's power

Ferdinand Marcos, elected to the presidency in 1965, ruled the Philippines for almost 20 years. A shrewd politician, Marcos built a power base supported by the military and financed by his government's stifling hold over the national economy.

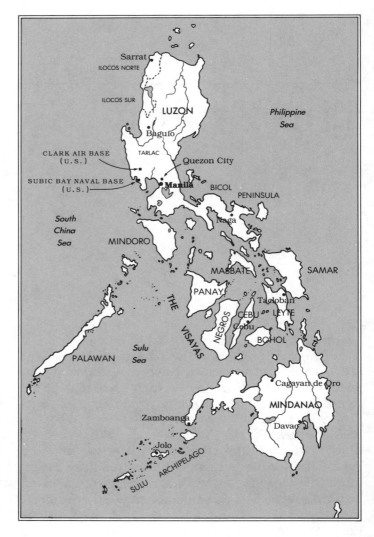

The Philippines is an archipelago in the south Pacific composed of more than 7,100 islands, many of which are so small they are not even named. Several different cultures, including native Malay, Spanish, Chinese, and American, have influenced the country.

It was a tragic outcome to an amazing career. The son of a teacher and a politician, Marcos was born in Sarrat, on the rugged Ilocos coast in northern Luzon. In 1939 he was found guilty of assassinating his father's political rival. In several court appeals, the 22-year-old law student, appearing in his own defense, established a national reputation for rhetorical brilliance and ingenious, biting argument. When the national bar examinations came around in the midst of his court appearances, Marcos boasted that he would place first. After he did, he successfully defended himself against ensuing charges of cheating. In 1940 the Philippine Supreme Court (perhaps more out of admiration than strict jurisprudence) overturned the lower court verdict. Marcos became a celebrity.

After World War II, Marcos boasted that he had led a guerrilla band against the Japanese occupation army, and he would later show off more than a score of medals he claimed he won for military valor. In the last years of his presidency, however, the bulk of these awards proved to have been fabricated by Marcos. Indeed, Marcos's father was executed by guerrillas for collaborating with the Japanese, and Marcos himself may have bartered equipment with the Japanese Imperial Army. In any event, the young lawyer exploited his war stories and his reputation for intellectual sharpness into successful runs for congressman, senator, and in 1965, after a costly and bitter election, president of the Philippines. With his beautiful, popular wife, Imelda Romualdez, Marcos moved into Malacañang Palace.

When Marcos came to power, the Philippines was one of the most rapidly industrializing and progressive countries of the Far East. However, a strong emphasis on industrial growth since the 1950s had meant that agricultural development suffered. Because of the country's colonial past, a land tenure system had evolved in which huge, modern plantations were worked by tenant farmers (or, in places, hired laborers) in the traditional way. Instead of educating the peasants to improve farming methods to raise productivity, the government merely increased the amount of land under cultivation in order to reap more profits. A policy of artificially controlled food prices to provide cheap food for the urban workers also hurt the farmers. When the chief Philippine export crops — sugar, timber, coconuts, and grains — began a steady decline in the 1960s, it only meant more misery for the peasant farmers. Those who still owned land were pushed off to provide more acreage for plantations, and the tenant farmers sank deeper into poverty. An enormous chasm widened between the upper and lower classes. Unemployment and underemployment were

During the 1950s, Philippine agriculture was neglected in the frenzied rush to develop industry. The grossly unfair and inadequate system of tenant farming, a legacy of the country's colonial past, meant lives of relentless poverty for the rural peasants.

Imelda Marcos (left) tours Detroit's Institute of Arts with Christina Ford. Imelda Marcos's frequent trips abroad, shopping excursions, and extensive building projects were a severe drain on the Philippine treasury, but she insisted that Filipinos expected their first lady to live in grand style.

rampant, and, by the late 1960s, the Philippines had the most lethargic economy of the Asian-Pacific nations. A land-reform program was desperately needed. But political power remained in the hands of the landed gentry, whose members made up the conservative legislatures. This ruling elite ensured the status quo of the agricultural system and the overprotection of the Philippine industries they owned.

Despite some early successes, the Marcos government created a severe economic crisis in the Philippines that defied any easy solutions. During his first two terms in office, Marcos initiated several vast projects that required massive government spending, including energy programs, self-sufficiency projects, and the industrial development of the southern island of Mindanao. But the Marcos policy of financing all kinds of domestic programs with huge foreign loans increased the national debt. As the government deficits grew, Marcos acquired more and more foreign loans at high interest rates. He gave the loans to his political supporters, his cronies, to finance their projects. Indeed, the economic system under Marcos has been termed "crony capitalism." When many of his cronies badly mismanaged their finances, Marcos bailed them out with additional foreign loans.

In November 1969, Marcos became the only Filipino to win a second presidential term. By January 1970, however, the tide was turning against him. Militant students pelted the Marcoses with rocks and bottles as they left the national legislature, forcing the couple to bolt themselves inside Malacañang. Four days later, 15,000 demonstrators attempted to storm the palace, lobbing Molotov cocktails on to the grounds before police broke up the riot. In the next two years, public order declined dramatically.

Meanwhile, Marcos, forbidden a third term by law, watched as Benigno Aquino prepared for a successful run for the presidency. Calling Aquino an unacceptable leftist, Marcos considered nominating either Imelda or Defense Secretary Enrile as his candidate against Aquino. However, polls indicated that Filipinos gave Imelda and Enrile little chance of succeeding against the charismatic Benigno.

The full extent of Imelda Marcos's shopping sprees did not become known until 1986. The many purchases she made with government revenues included more than 2,500 pairs of shoes.

Marcos acted decisively. In September 1972, citing the collapse of public order, including an attempt (staged, as it turned out) on the life of Enrile, Marcos extended his own political career by imposing martial law. In a crackdown carefully planned by Marcos's cousin General Fidel Ramos and Enrile, Aquino and thousands of other opponents of the regime were arrested. The free Philippine press was shut down, all firearms were confiscated, and a dawn-to-dusk curfew was imposed. Backed by a military he spoiled with favors and with the fruits of corruption, Marcos ruled by decree for the next 13 years. Later, he filled the ranks of the armed forces with friends, including General Fabian Ver, a distant relative and former chauffeur. Through Ver and his intricate military surveillance and spy network, Marcos kept a tight grip on all aspects of Filipino life, keeping one step ahead of his enemies and remaining master of the Philippines.

At first, Marcos's methods produced positive results. The tiny communist insurgency was stymied. The military quelled a bloody separatist movement by the country's Muslim minority, the Moros, in the southern islands. Meanwhile, the middle class, finally rid of gun-toting hoods and student riots, went back to work and, as a result, the Philippine economy made some gains from 1973 to 1977. If Marcos had dismantled martial law by 1977, said Enrile, "he would have been enshrined as the best president the country ever had." However, Marcos decided to hold on to power.

A rare family portrait of the Marcos family shows the president and first lady (center) surrounded by their children and grandchildren in 1986. Rumors circulated that the Marcoses were loathe to give up power because they intended to establish a presidential dynasty.

During the first years of martial law, Marcos tried to reduce government spending, but the economy continued on its downward spiral. In 1974, inflation in the Philippines reached its highest level since World War II. Marcos continued to finance his cronies with government money; monopolies in the sugar, coconut, and grain industries ensured lives of misery for the tenant farmers; and the foreign debt had reached a staggering sum. However, the extensive waste of the government's money was not limited to Marcos and his cronies alone.

Imelda, whom Marcos married after an 11-day courtship in 1954, had at first been shy about delving into politics. But her husband was well aware of the public relations advantages of a beautiful wife. She attracted the crowds, and her rags-to-riches story made her popular with many Filipinos. She grew to love politics intensely and later became second only to her husband in influence over the islands.

Imelda embarked on her own personal and public building projects: huge cultural centers, luxury hotels, and, in secret, private palaces for herself and her family. She abused government privileges by

A mother in the slums of Manila feeds her children. Shortly after his reelection in 1970, Marcos made the preposterous announcement that he would donate all his own money to help alleviate the abject poverty in which most Filipinos lived.

flying the national airlines on shopping trips to New York City and Europe. She hobnobbed with European aristocrats, American millionaires, and international movie stars. She bought property and jewelry wherever she went. She defended these extravagances by claiming that the Filipino people expected elegance from their star first lady: It showed how far a humble Filipina could go in the world. "I am both star and slave," she cooed.

Unfortunately, the projects Imelda built to serve her countrymen were mostly ostentatious displays of little practical use. The capital city acquired hospitals with luxury suites and the latest medical equipment, but the vast majority of Filipinos could not afford to stay in them. Manila's poor were hidden away in walled-off slums. Some were driven out to provide land for golf courses offered by the luxury five-star hotels that were built to promote tourism. Along Manila Bay, a huge reclamation project produced land to hold such attractions as the enormous stone and glass Philippine Cultural Center and the Philippine Folk Art Center, which was erected so the country could host the 1974 Miss Universe Pageant. The lavish "Coconut House," with its chandeliers and expensive murals, was hurriedly built to house Pope John Paul II on his Asian tour of 1981. The mansion was reportedly built entirely out of coconut products — coconut being a mainstay crop — to show the Filipinos what could be done with their natural resources. When the pope refused to stay in the Coconut House, the Marcoses had American model Brooke Shields host its opening instead. Imelda's penchant for ostentatious luxury became a constant target for Marcos's critics. Indeed, after the Marcoses' fall from power, Imelda's huge collection of shoes became symbolic of gross self-indulgence and excess.

Marcos arranged for his favorites to control most of the nation's wealth. His friends siphoned profits from huge national corporations into secret Marcos accounts in Switzerland and elsewhere. When the companies went bankrupt, Marcos came to the rescue with government bailouts that were funded with

The soldiers came and told us we must stay away from the land behind our village because Imelda's family wanted to put a cattle ranch there. . . . Then one day they came again when my neighbor was cutting wood on that land. They didn't give us any warning. They killed him with a machine gun. They came to my house and strafed it.
—Peasant woman on Leyte, Imelda Marcos's home island, 1984

foreign loans, some of which may have ended up in Marcos accounts as well. After Marcos was overthrown, Philippine officials estimated that his family and his cronies had amassed close to $10 billion.

In order to maintain her extravagant life-style, Imelda became more involved in politics, becoming almost as powerful as the president himself. While her foreign shopping sprees were paid for by the national treasury, in the countryside and in the cities three-quarters of the country languished in crushing poverty. Dispirited by the widening gap between the country's rulers and the lowest social classes, starving farmers and the urban poor proved to be a fruitful source of recruits for a reviving communist insurgency. From 1972 to 1985 the New People's Army (NPA), the Maoist military arm of the Philippine Communist party, grew from a ragtag band of a few hundred to a force of close to 20,000. To combat this threat, the Philippine military conducted raids in the countryside. Operating largely on their own, the government soldiers showed less and less regard for human rights, and they became a feared and despised force.

The naval station at Subic Bay is one of two U.S. military bases in the strategically located Philippines. Marcos's support of U.S. interests in southeast Asia earned him millions of dollars in aid.

California governor Ronald Reagan and his wife, Nancy, dance with the Marcoses during a 1969 goodwill tour of the Philippines. As U.S. president, Reagan staunchly supported the dictator despite Marcos's flagrant violations of human rights.

Despite the decline of his country's fortunes, Marcos continued to thrive as the source of all political power. But he was no longer the idealistic visionary who came to power in 1965. Instead, he was the prophet of a false democracy in a false republic. Proclaiming a policy of "constitutional authoritarianism," he set up a charter to legitimize his rule under a thin veneer of democratic principles. With a corrupting system of patronage, Marcos reached into every village in the country with the machinery of his monolithic party, the New Society Movement. To shield himself from foreign critics, Marcos cast their negative remarks as aspersions on Filipino nationalism. By imprisoning the most potent voices of the opposition, he prevented the rise of a viable rival. Furthermore, to foster the myth of his irreplaceability, he refused to name a successor and abolished the office of vice-president.

Marcos clung to power with such vehemence that he ignored his own failing health, perhaps believing that he had the will to cheat even death of victory. Rumors spread that he had undergone kidney operations and that he suffered from systemic lupus erythematosus, a disease that slowly destroys the internal organs. He knew the country would collapse into chaos if he died suddenly, without an heir, and yet he refused to give up control. Instead, he kept his medical condition a secret so as not to allow anyone a measure of power over him. Malacañang

Palace became a fortress and all approaches to it were blocked off from ordinary Filipinos. Planes were not allowed to fly over the palace lest they endanger the president's security. Every government appointment and every major business deal was in some way approved by the president.

His control over local politics made him indispensable to the United States, which was worried about its declining influence in Southeast Asia after the fall of Saigon in 1975 ended the Vietnam War. Almost to the end of Marcos's reign, concern for the sprawling and strategic American bases — the air base at Clark Field and the naval station at Subic Bay — was paramount in American policy regarding the Philippines. Clark and Subic straddled the vital sea lanes between Japan and Korea and the oil-rich Persian Gulf and faced the Soviet base of Cam Ranh Bay in Vietnam. Intent on preserving the American installations on Luzon island against either an anti-American or communist-dominated Manila, successive U.S. administrations from Lyndon Johnson to Ronald Reagan backed Marcos with more than $2 billion in military and economic funding over the dozen years of his dictatorship. Indeed, after Marcos staged a reelection for himself in 1980, U.S. vice-president George Bush traveled to Manila to toast the dictator's "adherence to democratic principles."

In a country that recalled its 40 years as an American colony with much fondness and sported strong cultural ties with its former colonial master, U.S. support was crucial for any Filipino leader. Most Filipinos believed that the United States would brook no other ruler save Marcos. Thus the United States was inextricably linked in the popular mind not to the Philippines as a country but to the Marcos dictatorship. Bolstered by Filipino acquiescence, U.S. aid, and a personal friendship with President Ronald Reagan, Marcos sat confidently in Malacañang, turning down all calls for reform with pedantic arguments and withering hauteur. Cardinal Sin called Marcos "a man who believes he is the only intelligent human being in the world."

BENIGNO S. AQUINO JR.
"NINOY"
NOV. 27, 1932 — AUG. 21, 1983

4
Taking Up the Mantle

A friend once asked Corazon Aquino what question she would put to Ferdinand Marcos if the shy housewife had a chance to speak to the dictator. The widow's reply was a quick and uncompromising accusation: "Why was Ninoy killed?"

Almost immediately after her husband's death, Aquino was on the offensive against Ferdinand Marcos. Unlike previous criticisms of the regime, Aquino's attack on Marcos was not simply one politician pointing out the shortcomings of another, but one of moral outrage. She disavowed any attempt by the Marcos government to find justice for her husband, and she blamed Marcos personally for the assassination.

Although she spoke out against Marcos soon after her return to Manila, at the beginning it was out of duty as a widow. Two months after the assassination, Aquino was still tentatively feeling out the boundaries of the immense influence and popularity that had been suddenly thrust upon her. After her husband's funeral, Aquino did little more than grace opposition rallies, say a few words about Ninoy, and read short, emotional speeches. On September 21, 1983, a month after the assassination,

Mr. Marcos is the No. 1 suspect in the murder of my husband.
—CORAZON AQUINO

Corazon Aquino visits her husband's grave in December 1985. Although she resisted popular pressure to run for public office, Aquino found herself the focus of a grass roots opposition campaign that proved hard to ignore.

she appeared before thousands of people gathered on the anniversary of the imposition of martial law. All she did, however, was thank her late husband's supporters and read sections of an anti-Marcos declaration.

Yet everyone else seemed to be demonstrating against Marcos. The business district of Makati, formerly a bastion of support for the regime, was suddenly inundated with unending parades of yellow, the color of resistance against the Marcos regime. Yellow t-shirts and pins and banners demanded Marcos's resignation. Although she steadfastly remained in the background, Aquino soon began directing the course of protest marches. In October 1983, fearing that government agents might infiltrate the crowd and cause trouble, Aquino advised that a demonstration attended by 10,000 women avoid the Mendiola Bridge, which led into Malacañang Palace. These women — local civic leaders, housewives, and mothers — were her first and strongest supporters. At their rally, she was surprised to hear people putting forward her name as the leader of the opposition and a candidate for president. Not accustomed to the limelight, she immediately dampened suggestions that she enter politics.

Filipinos, however, sensed the difference Aquino's presence made. Two weeks after Benigno's funeral, one woman wrote her nephew in Chicago of the events in Manila: "There was an air of intense sorrow and yet again an electrifying exultation of oneness, a joy of belonging to each other, in a common outrage, a common indignation, a common determination. . . . We are all standing ten feet tall. History is in the making here."

The same words were being uttered throughout the archipelago. Aquino was not unaware of it. But while the politicians who surrounded her saw the situation as an opportunity to rock the seat of Marcos's power, Aquino felt that politics was still an onerous and difficult task. To take up her husband's mantle, she would have to convince herself that it was entirely a matter of accepting God's will. Slowly, she came to believe it was.

In prison, Benigno had discovered a deep Christian faith that sustained him through the psychological and sometimes physical abuse inflicted on him. To Aquino, her husband's religious transformation became a symbol for the conversion that Philippine politics would have to undergo. That was the meaning Ninoy's suffering and death would have to have.

Her first task was to define Ninoy's work. She claimed him for the church, preempting any attempts by radical leftists to remake him in their own image. In a speech on March 10, 1984, Corazon wove into her husband's life the religious themes that she would use to win the hearts of her countrymen: spiritual resurrection, transformation, the triumph of good over evil. "When Ninoy emerged from prison," she said, "it seemed clear to those who knew him that much had changed in him. The superb political animal . . . had evolved into a man for whom love of country was only the other face of his love for God. And I think this is the truest and best kind of patriotism."

She belittled political solutions and recommended instead the power of faith to magnify men and women and inflame them with the strength to change the nation. By explaining to everyone the reasons behind Ninoy's greatness, she became his prophetess in the transfiguration of the Philippine body politic. Perhaps unwittingly, she became the first among those transformed by Ninoy's faith in the people.

People were galvanized by her piety. Hardened politicos and tough-minded businessmen were touched by her honesty, sincerity, and devotion to her husband. Like all Filipinos who heard her, they wept when she spoke, unable to hold back their emotions and their anger at themselves for tolerating a dictatorship. Aquino stood apart from the run-of-the-mill politicians. A figure of unassailable moral power, she genuinely tried to shun public adulation. But circumstances forced her to accept the idea of running for public office.

When Marcos announced that elections for the national legislature would be held in May 1984, the

WE ARE YOUR MOTHERS, WIVES, DAUGHTERS & SISTERS

Corazon Aquino (center) joins other women, including her mother-in-law, Aurora Aquino (right), at an anti-Marcos rally in October 1983. Aquino often attended opposition demonstrations but only, she claimed, as the widow of Benigno, not as a politician in her own right.

Aquino family split over their next move. Aquino was thrust into her first political fight — within her husband's family. Though there had been incidents of widows carrying on their husband's political careers, the most important precedents had been of younger brothers picking up the mantle of their older brothers. The Aquino family, some observers believed, felt that Benigno's younger brother Agapito "Butz" Aquino should run for office or at least make the crucial political decisions. Butz Aquino decided to support a movement boycotting the elections. Corazon chose to back the elections. The polls would decide whether Corazon or Butz would become the dominant political voice of the Aquinos.

Though she once shied away from political activism, Corazon campaigned tirelessly for the opposition candidates, traveling through rainstorms and over rocky highways to distant villages and faraway provinces. She claimed that the opposition parties could make a difference if they won enough contests. Butz Aquino, who became identified more and more with the leftist liberals, campaigned just as tirelessly and much more flamboyantly for a boycott. He claimed that Marcos would never allow the opposition significant victories.

The election results stunned Butz. The opposition took a third of the assembly seats and earned new credibility. Marcos gained little: Even though he "allowed" his rivals to win some seats, the public perception was that he cheated them of more. It was a strategic victory for the opposition, setting up a small but viable anti-Marcos power base that could be used as a launching pad for greater power bids. Her political stance vindicated, Corazon Aquino had won her first big victory.

By early 1985 Aquino had overcome any inclination in her family toward her brother-in-law's stewardship of Ninoy's legacy. However, she continued to deny that she would run for political office. In a February 1985 interview at a Makati building owned by the Cojuangcos, she stressed that her main concerns were still those of a "typical housewife." She spoke at length of her mastery of the secrets of roasting Peking duck and bemoaned the fact that Philippine duck lacked the fat to make good crackling.

Since late 1984 Corazon had been seeking ways to unify the fractious Philippine opposition, which was made up of half a dozen political parties. The

The opposition to Marcos was hindered by a lack of unity among the party leaders. Eva Estrada Kalaw, a prominent member of the Liberal party, was among the opposition presidential hopefuls.

Aquilino Pimentel, a popular congressman who had been jailed repeatedly by Marcos, addresses an antigovernment rally in 1985. The opposition leaders finally came to realize that no one except Aquino commanded the broad popular support necessary to oust Marcos.

opposition was split into three major divisions. The conservatives were represented by Salvador Laurel and the party he founded, the United Nationalist Democratic Organization party (UNIDO). Since 1978 the moderates had participated in the tentative coalition called *Lakasing Bayan* — People Power — which was known by its acronym, Laban. Laban offered the general approach of nonviolent, democratic means to power that Aquino seemed to favor. The leftist liberal-democrats, represented by Butz Aquino and the Coalition of Organizations for the Restoration of Democracy (CORD), unlike the other two groups, adopted an anti-American stand and demanded the removal of the U.S. bases. The communists of the New People's Army, continuing their military struggle in the countryside, remained outside the largely middle-class opposition movement.

By early 1985, the pressure on Aquino to run for president had become enormous. She immediately brought up practical arguments against it. She knew all about the petty jealousies and backroom maneuvering in Philippine politics. Candidates she did not endorse during the 1984 legislative elections would choose not to campaign for her, she believed. Too many other, more experienced people wanted to run for president. Salvador Laurel was quickly building up UNIDO as a powerful, organized party. The venerable Jovito Salonga, a veteran politician with a reputation for honesty, was one of the most beloved of Marcos's opponents. A score of others vied for prominence: Eva Estrada Kalaw, who led a powerful faction within the Liberal party; former congressman Ramón Mitra; prominent opposition leader Aquilino Pimentel; even her brother-in-law Butz Aquino. Not one of them, however, seemed to have the power to unite the opposition. They quarreled among themselves and plotted against each other. Filipinos looked upon all of them as politicians interested only in gaining power and influence for themselves. The people believed that not one of these opposition leaders had a good enough chance against Marcos. They knew Marcos would not give up power without a terrible fight.

Thus, the tribulations of a campaign for the presidency, a path Benigno could have easily mastered and relished, made Corazon Aquino cringe. There was no guarantee that "the good guys" would last even if they managed the seemingly impossible task of ousting Marcos. Benigno had predicted that whoever succeeded Marcos would face so many problems that he would be forced out of office within six months. Fearful of losing another member of her family to a political assassin, Aurora Aquino was concerned about the suggestions that her daughter-in-law run for office, and Aquino's own children opposed the idea. Whenever the subject came up, she always reaffirmed her decision to reject public office.

Aquino, at a 1985 memorial held on Benigno's birthday, announces that she is considering a presidential run. Still undecided, Aquino imposed two requirements for her candidacy — a snap election and a million signatures petitioning her to run.

In November 1985, under pressure from the United States to restore calm to the Philippines, Marcos announced that a snap presidential election would take place in February 1986. Here he talks to reporters after the announcement.

Still, by the second anniversary of Benigno's death, the leading opposition papers were beginning to describe Corazon Aquino as "presidential." Readers filled columns with letters begging her to run for president. Letty Jimenez-Magsanoc, editor of the top-selling alternative paper *Mr. & Ms.*, wrote, "She was poised without being snobby; proper without being coy; spontaneous without being impulsive; natural without being anxious; one's everyday Filipino housewife without being dreary. . . . Today, Ninoy might well be known as Cory Aquino's husband." Questioned about the possibility that the opposition might draft her as its presidential candidate against her wishes, Aquino replied wittily, "There is no such thing as a draft in this country. Only typhoons."

Aquino was not without detractors. As a prominent moderate leader, she was the object of verbal attacks by the procommunist left in the opposition. The radicals argued that all she sought to do was make Marcos behave properly. They criticized "Mrs. Corazon (Cory) Aquino's statement that all we can do is pray that Marcos will change." She did not allow the left to use that apparent weakness against her for long. By October 1985 she had abandoned any hope of reconciliation with Marcos. As the dictator continued to ruin the Philippines and as the opposition continued to bicker, Aquino slowly began to think seriously of running for the presidency. There seemed to be no other way to fulfill Ninoy's dreams.

A Roman Catholic priest blesses the million signatures collected to support Aquino's candidacy. Before making her decision to enter the race, Aquino went into seclusion to pray for help in making the right choice. Once she believed that it was God's will, she emerged determined to run.

In mid-October 1985, without her approval, the Draft Cory Aquino for President Movement was launched. The movement was spearheaded by Joaquin Roces, a newspaper publisher who had been Benigno's first boss. In an emotional statement, he voiced the conviction held by many people that Aquino was the leader the country needed.

Aquino had consciously kept out of the public eye, but her low profile did not lessen the clamor for her candidacy. She now sought to make her running for office impossible by attaching two difficult requirements to it. First, Marcos had to call a "snap" election, that is, one held before the designated time; second, petitions for the Draft Cory Aquino for President Movement would have to be signed by 1 million Filipinos. She would run only if both conditions were met.

Aquino was convinced that neither condition would be fulfilled. However, the United States, concerned about its military bases in the islands, was pressing Marcos to reform his government. A greater amount of democracy, the U.S. government felt, might alleviate the Filipinos' anger against Marcos and slow down the growth of the communist New People's Army, which was waging an increasingly successful guerrilla war. On November 3, 1985, after a series of meetings with U.S. officials, Marcos announced that he would hold a snap presidential election to prove that he was still the man Filipinos wanted as president.

At almost the same time, over 1 million signatures had been collected, urging Cory Aquino to run. Shocked at how quickly her conditions had been met, Aquino went into seclusion at a convent to pray for guidance. A few days later, she said to Cardinal Sin, "Ninoy is inspiring me. It seems he is talking to me, telling me that I should run." Though he was known to favor Aquino's candidacy, the cardinal asked her to consider her decision carefully. "It is not a joke to go against Marcos," he said.

Despite the public clamor for her candidacy, the decision to run did not come easily to Corazon. She pondered the possible obstacles with pollsters, politicians, and economists gathered together by her

> *I always say that no revolution can be won unless there is first a revolution within the individual person, a revolution of the heart.*
> —JAIME CARDINAL SIN

brother, former Tarlac congressman Jose Cojuang-co. However, they could provide only limited statistical studies of possible voting patterns; the experts could not give her a direction. "Do the people," she asked, "understand abstract things like truth, justice, and freedom that I always talk about or do they only understand material things? I have the impression that if elections are held, we are lost, because only Marcos can give them rice and pesos." They had no answers for her.

Her answer came during a visit to Manila Memorial Park, the cemetery where members of her family, including Benigno, were buried. Aquino brought her dilemma to the local priest, who told her that the candidate had to be the complete opposite of Marcos. For Filipinos to identify with the candidate, the person should be "someone who has been a victim." She was convinced. "Looking around, I may not be the worst victim," she said, "but I am the best known."

Aquino returned to the cardinal at the beginning of December: "I am now sure to run. It is God's will." The cardinal blessed her and said, "You will win. You are our Joan of Arc." Corazon Aquino prepared for battle.

Cardinal Sin's wholehearted support was vital to Aquino's decision to run. In a country as deeply religious as the Philippines, the backing of the Catholic church was essential for the success of any candidate.

5

The Candidate

For 20 years," Corazon Aquino said at a press conference in early December 1985, "we have had one of the most brilliant Filipinos as president, and yet look what happened. Our country has been devastated." As photographers snapped their cameras and reporters recorded her words, everyone in the room knew what was happening. Aquino was responding positively to the months of heated appeals. She was about to run for president.

She timed her announcement well. For two years after Benigno's death, Aquino had kept her distance from the fact-finding board Marcos appointed to investigate her husband's murder. She continued to distance herself even after the majority of the board announced that Benigno had been murdered by his military escort and not by a lone communist gunman, as Marcos had argued. When General Fabian Ver was put on trial as part of the military conspiracy that murdered Benigno, Aquino predicted that,

On election day, bring two pieces of bread and a bottle of water. Bring a candle too. . . . If you think these will not do, bring a 2-by-2 piece of wood and protect your ballot with it.
—SALVADOR LAUREL
Aquino's running mate, to voters before election

Candidates Corazon Aquino and Salvador Laurel pose in front of a portrait of Benigno. The most discouraging problem Aquino faced after declaring her candidacy was posed by Laurel, an experienced politician with presidential ambitions of his own. The sometimes bitter negotiations between Aquino and Laurel almost destroyed the opposition campaign before it began.

Aquino files for her candidacy, December 1985. Her reconciliation with Laurel and their agreement to run under Laurel's party, UNIDO, occurred so late that their candidacy was officially registered only minutes before the deadline.

as a Marcos subordinate, he would emerge without punishment. A Philippine court cleared General Ver after ignoring eyewitness accounts and damaging testimony against him and a score of other alleged conspirators. Filipinos were outraged. A day after the court announced its decision, Corazon Aquino announced her candidacy for the presidency of the Philippines.

Though Aquino was greatly respected by a large number of Filipinos, her candidacy was faced with a host of problems. She was unsure whether she could unite the opposition groups, and the selection of a vice-president from among them posed a particularly thorny problem. She feared that her inexperience would be a great hindrance. Filipinos were accustomed to the crafty, much more politically sophisticated Marcos. The absolute grip Marcos held over the country was yet another consideration. The president controlled the media and commanded more wealth than Aquino had at her disposal. He could prevent her from getting any coverage and simply buy all the votes he needed.

Finally, there was the question of opposition from her own side. Salvador Laurel had been in the Marcos opposition for years and would not easily give up his meticulously planned drive for the presidency. Indeed, Laurel posed a personal problem for Aquino. Though he had been one of Benigno's friends, "Doy" Laurel was never one of Corazon's favorites. He was the quintessential Filipino politico: dashing and debonair, glib and eloquent, equal parts charm and deceit. Because there were so many more qualified candidates, Aquino was afraid that she would be accused of using the people's sentiments to gain a position of power she had not earned.

Although Laurel was well organized and charismatic, he had liabilities. During martial law, while the other opposition members were being rounded up and locked into jails, Laurel's political connections managed to prevent his arrest. For a while, Laurel even joined Marcos's ruling party, the New Society Movement, which ultimately marred his credibility. People whispered that ambition, not moral disagreement, was the chief reason Laurel distanced himself from Marcos and founded UNIDO; Marcos's party was too full of presidential hopefuls — Imelda, Enrile, and others — and Laurel, rumor had it, felt it would be better to strike out on his own.

Filipinos viewed Laurel's association with Marcos as unsavory, but they admired him for his ability to weld a political party second in effectiveness only to the president's own machine. Yet, despite the ties he built with the opposition and his personal connection to Benigno, Laurel's political behavior reminded many of the master of Malacañang. Rumors that Marcos liked the kind of opposition represented by Laurel did not boost either man's standing among the people.

Though she would later learn to appreciate some of his political talents, Aquino did not like the way Laurel tried to manipulate politics from behind the scenes, conniving and plotting to trip up rivals. In an interview in February 1985 Aquino said Laurel

Marcos crony General Fabian Ver was among the 26 men charged with the murder of Benigno Aquino. It was widely believed that the Marcos government tampered with evidence, ignored crucial testimony, and threatened eyewitnesses in order to absolve Marcos of any responsibility.

In December 1985 a judge acquitted all the defendants on trial for Benigno's killing, including General Ver. Outraged Filipinos took to the streets, and in a perfectly timed maneuver, Aquino declared her candidacy the following day.

had approached her and asked her to run as his vice-president if an election was called. He knew that Aquino's enormous moral appeal to the Filipinos would make his own candidacy more attractive if she ran as his vice-president. However, Laurel clearly wanted her to be nothing more than a figurehead. He had been known to say that he did not think the Philippines was ready for a "lady president." Dealing with the problems of Laurel's ambitions and the place of UNIDO would almost scuttle Aquino's campaign before it began.

Aquino was also worried about the mudslinging that occurred so frequently in Philippine politics. Though she had no political career to speak of and, thus, no damaging political background, her relatives were extremely politicized and would be easy targets for those wishing to tarnish her reputation. Aquino had little qualms about her in-laws. The Aquinos were to a great degree transfigured by the martyrdom of Benigno, though Butz was believed to be too headstrong and too leftist for his own good. Aquino was afraid, however, that her own family, the Cojuangcos, might prove to be less than an asset in the election.

Specifically, Aquino feared that people might say she was running only because of an old family feud. Her cousin Eduardo Cojuangco was a very close ally of the Marcos family and was considered by some to be the president's secret successor. He had split with the Cojuangco clan in the 1960s after contesting a bitter election in Tarlac with Corazon's brother Jose.

The divided Cojuangcos battled over control of Tarlac, then contested national politics: Eduardo supported Marcos whereas Jose supported Benigno Aquino. In the early 1970s Jose held the upper hand, but their fortunes were reversed under martial law. Now Jose Cojuangco was supporting his sister, armed with Benigno's legacy, to take back what was once almost his. Aquino was concerned about the vicious political rumors. Why should the 70 percent of the country that was poor support Corazon Aquino if they felt she was merely her family's instrument in a squabble among the unscrupulous rich?

Perhaps Aquino's worst liability was the issue of her own identity. One Manila columnist went so far as to say that she was merely a symbol of the anti-Marcos movement without any substance of her own — "a woman with no political biography." Marcos himself had put forward that argument. Scoffing at the idea of being challenged by a housewife, he muttered that a housewife's place was at home.

It was a personal dilemma for Aquino. She had often called her husband a "male chauvinist" and knew that he probably would not have approved of her candidacy — or for that matter, of any woman candidate, but it was the only way she knew to make his dreams come true. She did not help her cause by blurting out such reflections as "What in the world do I know about being president?" She may have thought that by modestly putting herself down, she was making herself as different as possible from the man she hoped to replace. But to many Filipinos, her words seemed to indicate that she knew nothing about politics, and worse, nothing about governing. Even foreign observers sympathetic to her cause were at first dismayed by her style and impolitic self-deprecation. "Naive," one American newspaper called her.

> *Look, let's admit it. She's being used by the people around her.*
> —FERDINAND MARCOS
> on Aquino's
> political naïveté

Aquino and Laurel campaign in the central province of Cebu. Nervous and inexperienced at the start, Aquino quickly gained confidence and ability as the campaign progressed.

So Aquino not only had to find a way around Marcos's control of the media and the very mechanics of election but also had to surmount some very basic problems: opposition politicians such as Laurel, less than sterling family relations, and a reputation for inexperience and naïveté. To anyone else, it might have seemed impossible. But Corazon Aquino had enormous strengths that towered above anything even Marcos possessed. She had her own quiet indomitability; she enjoyed a tremendous popularity with the Filipino people, and she had the unbending support of the powerful Roman Catholic church.

It was Cardinal Sin, spiritual leader of the country's 45 million Catholics, who finally healed the rift between Corazon and Laurel. On December 3, 1985, when Aquino declared her candidacy, Laurel, too, announced he would seek the presidency, thereby raising the specter of a Marcos victory by way of a split opposition vote. Earlier negotiations had broken down between Laban, which supported Aquino, and Laurel's UNIDO party.

During the negotiations, Laurel had acceded to Aquino's desire to run for the presidency. He was too good a politician to fail to recognize her popularity. He demanded, however, that she run as a "guest" candidate on his party slate, thereby guaranteeing UNIDO the status of ruling party if she won the election. Cory Aquino was adamant: She would not run under the UNIDO banner, and if Laurel did not come over to her side, she would refuse to consider him as a running mate. She believed she was to be the candidate of a new kind of politics, and her dislike of Laurel and politicians in his mold was obvious.

Laurel's UNIDO political machine was immense and crucial to bringing voters to the polls. Aquino's Laban supporters, though popular, were not quite as organized. Without Laurel, Aquino would be unable to win. Without Aquino's popularity, Laurel would just as easily be swamped by Marcos. Suddenly, after the excitement that greeted Aquino's decision to run, Filipinos gasped at how quickly their hopes were evaporating. As Aquino stood her ground, UNIDO began to crumble. Politicians allied with Laurel realized that Aquino was much more popular and defected to her side. The danger lay in the possibility that if UNIDO disintegrated, its organized ability to drum up votes for the opposition would disappear as well.

Imelda Marcos sings at a rally. Her husband's ill health made it difficult for him to campaign actively, so Mrs. Marcos addressed rallies, traveled to many of the provinces, and enlisted the support of celebrities to bring about his reelection.

Despite the argument that she was playing into Marcos's hands by dividing the opposition, Aquino refused to budge. Perhaps if she had her way, she would choose a politician who had suffered severely under Marcos, for example, Aquilino Pimentel, with whom Aquino had long said she was "comfortable." But others feared that Pimentel was too socialist. Already Marcos was saying that Corazon Aquino was merely a figurehead for the communists, who would seize power if she became president. A less traditional running mate than Laurel might prove disastrous, stripping her campaign of its crucial support from the centrist, anticommunist middle class. At this point, Cardinal Sin stepped in.

In most popular versions of the reconciliation, the cardinal told Laurel to give up his presidential bid simply because he could not match Aquino's attractiveness. Sin's greater achievement, however, was in convincing Aquino that, with UNIDO members defecting to her side, she had proven which of the two potential presidential candidates was "more attractive." Cardinal Sin explained to Aquino that she should not embarrass Laurel by destroying his

Presidential candidate Aquino dons a hat while campaigning in the rain on the island of Mindanao. Aquino personally brought her message of hope and her vision of change to nearly every one of the 73 Philippine provinces.

party. Aquino then acquiesced to Laurel's request that she run under UNIDO. The new team rushed out to the offices of the Commission of Elections and registered itself minutes before the midnight deadline for the filing of candidacies. With the formation of such a powerful team, minor contenders in the opposition threw their support to the Aquino-Laurel ticket.

To prevent the electoral cheating that many feared Marcos would stoop to in order to steal the election, the cardinal promoted the idea of a citizens' watch organization to monitor the vote. The National Movement for Free Elections (NAMFREL) had already ensured the election of many opposition politicians in the legislative contests of May 1984. It would prove crucially important in documenting the fraud and violence that would mar the February 1986 presidential election. The cardinal's support also emboldened the official Catholic radio station, Veritas, to broadcast coverage of the Aquino-Laurel campaign. Sin knew that most other radio and television stations would devote air time to Marcos and give scant attention to the opposition.

Anti-Marcos demonstrators destroy an effigy of the dictator on the barbed wire surrounding the presidential palace. From December 1985 to February 1986 the Philippines was gripped by the passions aroused by the election campaigns.

From December 10, 1985, to February 5, 1986, the Philippines was possessed by election mania. Marcos and Imelda spent freely, waging a slick campaign with music and movie stars. So-called rent-a-crowds were paid to swell Marcos rallies. Though Marcos himself seemed too sick to last through entire meetings, the old dictator put on a good show, blasting the opposition as "communist dummies" and reminding his audience that only he was smart enough and strong enough to keep anarchy from destroying the Philippines. Wherever he went, he signed decrees earmarking government money for the locality, and he made promises only the government could deliver.

At the rallies, Imelda, dressed in the red and blue official colors of the Marcos campaign, warmed up the crowds by singing traditional love songs and begging the people to love her husband as much as she did. At one rally, she stretched out her thumb and index finger in the "L" sign that the opposition used to signify Aquino's supporters in Laban (the acronym Laban also stood for the Filipino word for *fight*). As the audience gasped in shock, she turned the "L" on its side, her index finger, the barrel and her thumb, the trigger. "This is what the opposition is really trying to do," she said. In short, Marcos meant power and control over anarchy, Aquino meant chaos. Instead, the official Marcos hand sign was the American-style "V" for victory. That was what the Marcoses expected, and weeks before the election, Marcos's henchmen were boasting in private that they had already started to count the vote.

Aquino's campaign was not as well funded, but she worked harder than Marcos, whose health kept him close to the capital. Aquino toured practically every one of the country's 73 provinces. Her campaign platform rested more on emotions and broad agendas than on concrete programs. Aquino personified the new direction many wished to see the Philippines take. She told the people she wanted to end poverty and give the workers hope for a better life. She told businessmen she would seek to reestablish Philippine credibility in the international fi-

nancial community and attract foreign investments again. She declared that she would open reconciliation talks with the communist rebels in the countryside. She exhorted the Filipinos: "Think less of ourselves, think more of our country."

Marcos had a virtual monopoly over entertainment stars to attract an audience, and newspapers announced his arrival days in advance. Aquino had to depend on word of mouth to draw crowds. The political miracle was that Filipinos cared enough about her to give their time and lives in her service. Though terribly disorganized in the beginning, by the end of the campaign she was drawing millions. Crowds waited for hours in bad weather to see her. They came to draw strength from the hope she gave that change could take place, that Marcos could be ousted. She in turn came to draw strength from the people.

Her campaign was an extraordinary achievement. This woman, whose voice was at times little more than a squawk, drew hundreds of thousands to rallies. It was at such mass gatherings that she came

Aquino, Laurel, and supporters flash the "L" sign — for their Laban coalition — in front of a giant bust of Marcos. In spite of the fact that they were denied coverage by the Marcos-controlled media, Aquino and Laurel attracted millions of followers.

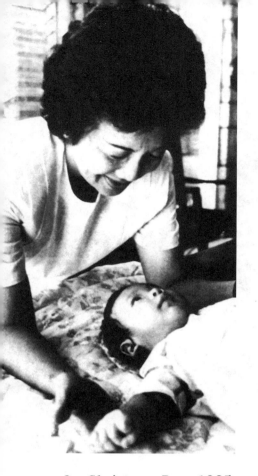

On Christmas Day, 1985, taking a well-deserved break from her campaign activities, Aquino plays with the grandson her husband never saw, Justin Benigno Aquino Cruz.

to realize the worth of Salvador Laurel. A talented politician, Laurel could make a crowd laugh at jokes or bristle with anger; he could amuse them with clever words and challenge them with strong rhetoric to think. He stirred them up and prepared them for Aquino, for her humble but irresistible emotional force. When it came time to make the audience weep, he wisely gave up the podium to "Cory" —the widow, the victim, the candidate.

The sad lyrics of the nationalist hymn *Bayan Ko* welled up almost automatically from the crowds. The haunting beauty of the song symbolized everything Corazon Aquino stood for: freedom from Marcos, from his oppression and injustice. To the thousands of ordinary people who gathered to hear her, the small woman in yellow with the unmelodious voice was a victim as surely as they were victims. In her later campaign speeches, Aquino crystallized her battle with Marcos into one of the oppressed against the oppressor, of a liberator against a tyrant, of good against evil.

Her campaign became a crusade, and the parallels between religious symbolism and reality were astounding. In a country as religious as the Philippines, such symbolisim could not but have had a galvanizing effect. Appropriately enough, the election colors broke down along biblical lines. The official color of Marcos's New Society Movement was red, the red of the satanic dragon of the Book of Revelation. Imelda Marcos often dressed in flaming red ternos, identifying her with the scarlet woman of Babylon, drunk with the blood of saints. The opposition, however, presented the most startling of transfigurations, a parallel to the "great wonder" of the 12th chapter of the book of Revelation: a self-confessed housewife dressed in yellow transformed by fate and circumstance into the apocalyptic "woman clothed with the sun" who would bring salvation to the world. Her speeches rang with fervor: "I say to Mr. Marcos what Moses said to the cruel enslaving pharaoh — Let our people go! The nation has awakened. I, like millions of Filipinos, look on this awakening as the dawning of a new day.

"I have seen the broken bodies of men, women, and children buried under promises of peace and progress. I have heard the anguished voices of the victims of injustice answered only by hypocritical pledges of retribution. I have been kissed by the poorest of the poor and have felt the warmth of their tears on my cheeks. . . . I have been electrified by their every cry for freedom, and inspired by their every clasp of hope. I cannot shut my ears to them. I cannot turn my back on them."

Support came from all over. The poor used the money they had earned begging as contributions to the campaign. Sidewalk food vendors fashioned their own campaign posters. Students drew up banners with paint and paper. Society ladies forsook their fancy restaurants and worked hand-in-hand with their servants to prepare for Aquino's travels. The country's leading intellectuals drew up Aquino campaign strategies and proposals for government reform and educated her on national problems. As she studied and learned, her critics found they could no longer fault her for näiveté. Even the leftists who boycotted the election, branding it as a fraud bound to be rigged by Marcos, voiced grudging admiration for Aquino.

Everyone was awed by her powerful presence. She always greatly inspired all those who saw and heard her. The candidate herself was amazed at her support and profoundly affected by the experience. An adviser recalled joking with Aquino on the way to visit the cardinal of Cebu, in the Visayan Islands, the central island group of the Philippines. Along the road, hundreds of thousands of people had gathered, waving yellow banners and shouting her name. "Cory," the adviser said, "perhaps you should ask the cardinal to forgive all his people here in Cebu." "Why?" she inquired. "They are beginning to commit the sin of idolatry," her adviser jokingly replied.

Election day — February 7, 1986 — finally arrived, after close to 60 days of campaigning. There had been many threats on Aquino's life. Her son-in-law, Eldon Cruz, Maria Elena's husband, accompanied

> *It will be an exceptionally fraudulent election. But the difference [between the candidates] is people will not only vote for Cory, they will die for her.*
> —BREN GUIAO
> former campaign manager
> for Benigno Aquino

her as a bodyguard. But she faced the threats calmly. She disliked large cordons of security men and preferred to be in a position where people could see her, reach her, and hear her. Everything, she believed, operated on God's time: Life was not hers to choose, only God's to give. To many people, this bravery was like Benigno's on the day he died.

Aquino often thought of Ninoy and what he was missing. Ninoy did not get to see Eldon and Maria Elena's wedding, the first among the Aquino children, which took place in 1984. He never saw their son, his grandson, Justin Benigno Aquino Cruz. He never saw the people gather in huge rallies to support his wife. He never saw any of these miraculous events.

Aquino learned quickly. She learned to take charge. At first she had mostly followed what her many advisers told her. But soon she was making the most important decisions in the campaign, holding it together with her calm and equanimity. She seemed able to make practical choices in the confusing election rush.

She reminded everyone, including the men who doubted her abilities, that she would do everything on her terms. "Some who support my candidacy say that if I am elected my role will be that of Mother of the Nation. . . . If elected I will remain a mother to my children, but I intend to be chief executive of this nation. And for the male chauvinists in the

Marcos and his vice-presidential running mate, Arturo Tolentino, acknowledge the crowd at a campaign rally in the northern Philippines. The ailing dictator was often reduced to hiring reluctant people to swell the numbers at his rallies.

audience, I intend as well to be the commander-in-chief of the armed forces of the Philippines." She was no longer a reluctant candidate. She had become an eminently confident one.

Three days before election day, Aquino called together a huge crowd for her final rally. In Manila, more than 500,000 (perhaps even 1 million) people appeared to hear her give her final speech. Again she asked them to pray. They sang *Bayan Ko* for Cory and for their beloved, suffering country. In contrast to Aquino's fervent crowds, Marcos's audiences were reluctant to stay. The president's men had to ship people into Manila for Marcos's final rally. But when rain fell, his crowds began to melt away. Some of the fleeing audience told reporters at the scene that they had been paid to attend but would vote for Aquino anyway.

On election day, Corazon Aquino dressed herself in yellow and prepared to vote in her hometown in Tarlac. She was filled with confidence that she had already won. She believed that she had obeyed God's will by running for the presidency. To reporters and photographers covering her, Aquino said, "This is my day. See you at my inaugural." But election day would turn into a nightmare. Marcos was not at all ready to concede.

In front of election posters and a UNIDO banner, Aquino makes a speech as her exhausting, exhilarating campaign winds down. Aquino had witnessed such fervent support among the Filipinos that she had no doubt that she would be elected to the presidency.

6

Apocalypse

Who was to be believed? First, Aquino made her announcement: "The trend is clear and irreversible. The people and I have won, and we know it. We are home again in a country we can call our own." Then Marcos went on the air nationwide. The results, he said, "indicate that I probably have won."

The polls had opened early on February 7, 1986. By 7 A.M., long lines of voters had formed outside schoolhouses throughout the country, ready to cast their ballots in what almost everyone in the islands knew would be the most important test of democracy in the country's history. All in all, 26 million Filipinos would vote.

Already, however, forces that would derail the democratic exercise were at work. Local officials belonging to the Marcos bureaucracy busily bought votes and organized small squads of "flying voters," who were bused from precinct to precinct to vote repeatedly for Marcos and his vice-presidential running mate, Arturo Tolentino. In the districts of Manila believed to be strongly pro-Aquino, voters

Once a champion, always a champion.
—FERDINAND MARCOS
claiming victory in the
1986 election

Corazon Aquino casts her vote on election day, February 7, 1986. Because the opposition feared that widespread cheating by the Marcos forces would rob them of victory, it monitored the election closely.

entered the polling areas only to discover that their names had disappeared from the official registration lists, so they could not vote. Perhaps 3 million people were prevented from voting in this way. Violence marred the election. Masked gunmen traveling in packs burst into polling booths and threatened the voters, then stole the ballot boxes. Television cameras of foreign correspondents recorded some of these incidences of fraud. An official observation team made up of U.S. congressmen, led by Missouri senator Richard Lugar, was aghast at the widespread cheating. In the United States, Georgia senator Sam Nunn asked the White House to terminate all aid to the Philippines if "the will of the voters, as expressed at the ballot box, is not followed." Even Marcos's friend, President Ronald Reagan, after being sharply criticized for saying that there "had been cheating on both sides," was forced to agree that the vote had been "marred by widespread fraud and violence perpetrated by the ruling party."

In the Philippines, the feelings were not only of outrage but of violation. Filipinos were disgusted by the barely disguised attempt to concoct a Marcos victory. Hundreds of thousands of volunteers had tried to ensure a fair election, handcarrying ballot boxes by way of human chains to vote-counting centers. At night, hundreds kept vigil to make sure that no one tampered with the vote. Still the government machine was too powerful. NAMFREL's unofficial vote showed Aquino ahead, but Marcos's Commission on Elections had the president leading. Two days after the election, 30 computer workers at the Commission's national vote-counting center walked out, charging that the numbers being posted for the public did not match the number of votes coming in. Aquino was cheated in almost every way. Finally, Marcos forced his victory by having the puppet National Assembly declare him the winner. The assembly's final count — 10,807,179 for Marcos and 9,491,716 for Aquino — was not taken seriously by anyone. Aquino warned the government that if she was cheated of her real victory, she would lead daily protest demonstrations.

As it became clear that Marcos had stolen victory from Aquino, the coalition of radical leftists known as *Bayan* — the National Democratic Alliance — and the communists cried, "We told you so!" They still advocated the path of violent revolution as the only way to remove Marcos. With the election in disarray, the communist guerrillas in the hills seemed to be the only force powerful enough to rid the country of the Marcos scourge. What Aquino needed to keep her followers from swinging to the communists was public and unambiguous support from the moral authority of almost all Filipinos, the Roman Catholic church.

Marcos had tried hard to prevent this. He sent Imelda to stop the country's bishops from condemning the election results. Corazon listened intently to the latest reports on the bishops' discussions, praying silently. Finally the bishops declared, "The people have spoken. Or have tried to. . . . In our considered judgment, the polls were unparalleled in the fraudulence of their conduct. . . . If [the] government does not of itself freely correct the evil it has inflicted on the people, then

Protesters burn a U.S. flag outside the American embassy in Manila. Because the United States had been a strong supporter of the Marcos regime, many Filipinos wanted the U.S. presence in the Philippines removed along with the widely hated dictator.

Lieutenant General Fidel Ramos secured the ultimate victory of Aquino when he provided crucial military support to anti-Marcos rebels. On February 22, 1986, Defense Minister Juan Ponce Enrile, Ramos, and a small group of soldiers barricaded themselves in camps on the outskirts of Manila.

it is our serious moral obligation as a people to make it do so."

When she heard the news, Imelda reportedly threw a fit and fell to the floor, babbling, in Cardinal Sin's office. A week after the election, Cardinal Sin made his position clear when he appeared at a mass wearing yellow robes. Aquino now felt that she could call out the people for massive nonviolent demonstrations against the regime.

Aquino wanted them to raise their voices in protest against Marcos and shatter his increasingly fragile hold. On February 16, she presided over a gigantic "Victory of the People" rally in Manila to announce her tactics of nonviolence. An economic boycott of all goods produced by companies owned by Marcos and his cronies was instituted. The stock market plunged immediately. Newspapers that once toadied to Marcos found their circulation figures cut dramatically. Filipinos even gave up their favorite beer, San Miguel, which was produced by a company controlled by Eduardo Cojuangco. Many Filipinos, however, wondered if peaceful tactics were enough to overthrow Marcos.

The wily president already had made plans to arrest Aquino, Cardinal Sin, and practically every major opposition leader and imprison them on the tiny, desolate island of Caballo in Manila Bay. But a danger lurked that even Marcos had not foreseen, and his discovery of it would throw the country into a crisis.

In Marcos's own party there were many ambitious politicians who had sacrificed their own careers while they served the president. Chief among them was Defense Minister Juan Ponce Enrile. He had been a Marcos protégé in the years before the president began his dictatorship. Enrile had diligently put together the plan to administer martial law throughout the country. Many felt that Enrile would be the most acceptable Marcos-style successor to the president. But the president was wary of all who thought they had a chance to succeed him. Enrile fell out of favor and saw his chances of becoming president fade as Imelda Marcos and General Fabian Ver gained more of the dictator's attention. But Enrile did not give up.

Catholic priests and nuns stand in the way of government tanks sent to overcome Enrile and the rebels at Camp Crame. When the military, refusing to fire on the crowds, defected to the rebel camp, Marcos's defeat was ensured.

Although military matters were under the control of General Ver (who was restored to his government post after being acquitted of Benigno Aquino's murder), Enrile still had strong support within the armed forces. He encouraged a secret organization of young officers who were dissatisfied with the corruption of Marcos's military and wanted to reestablish the professionalism of the Filipino soldier. Frustrated with trying to work through the system, they decided to take armed action against Marcos and Ver. The reformist officers planned to blow up Marcos's palace bodyguard, kill Ver's crack troops, capture Malacañang, and imprison the Marcos family. They would then install a ruling council that would represent the opposition and the church in the persons of Aquino and Cardinal Sin. But Enrile would head this military junta. Unfortunately for the general, Marcos found out about the planned coup, and he ordered the arrest of Enrile and his military supporters.

On February 22, 1986, at 9:00 P.M., a message came over the Veritas airwaves from Cardinal Sin to Filipinos: "I am sorry to disturb you at this late hour, but it is precisely at a time like this that we most need your support for our two good friends." The two good friends were Defense Minister Enrile and Lieutenant General Fidel Ramos. Three hours earlier they had defected from the Marcos regime and set up rebel headquarters on the edge of Manila at the military camps of Crame and Aguinaldo.

Surprised by the discovery of his planned coup and frightened by news that Marcos was about to arrest him, Enrile had earlier called General Ramos to join him. Ramos, a widely respected professional soldier, agreed immediately. Though Enrile was the instigator of the rebellion, he was barely trusted by most Filipinos because of his years of association with Marcos. Ramos, though a cousin of Marcos, was still considered the best hope of the military, and his presence would add considerable respectability to the mutiny. A good name, however, would not stop Marcos and Ver from launching an armed attack. Enrile and Ramos had only a few hundred men. Marcos had jets, attack helicopters, heavy artillery, and hundreds of thousands of troops at his command.

When Enrile told Cardinal Sin of his plight, Ramos suggested that the cardinal rally the people to the rebels' cause. The call went out, and tens of thousands of people came: clerics, nuns, and ordinary citizens bearing rosaries, crosses, the yellow banners of the opposition, and plaster statues of the Virgin Mother of God. Those who tuned in to the cardinal's later broadcasts remember that he spoke in language rich with allusions to Christian martyrdom, saying that the time had come for all true believers to bear witness for their faith. Hundreds of thousands filled Epifanio de los Santos Avenue (EDSA), the major route that ran between the camps, to show their support for Enrile and Ramos. In the days that followed, their rosary beads stopped tanks, their flowers subdued soldiers, their prayers forced helicopter gunships to defect from the Marcos military machine. They laid their bodies down in front of tanks headed for the mutineers. Throughout, they chanted the name that had echoed throughout the two-month election campaign: "Cory! Cory!"

When she heard the news of Enrile's mutiny, Aquino was in Cebu City, on the island of Cebu. Her advisers quickly brought her to a nearby convent to hide from Marcos's increasingly jittery soldiers. Over the phone she spoke to the cardinal, voicing her fear that Enrile and his military supporters were only trying to force themselves into power. After all, Enrile had been her husband's official jailer. She had no reason to trust him.

After the cardinal convinced Aquino that Enrile was on her side, she called Enrile at his camp. "What can I do for you?" she asked. "Just pray for us," the defense minister told her. As the situation became increasingly tense, Blaine Porter, the U.S. consul in Cebu, called to offer her refuge on a nearby U.S. ship. She politely refused, and the next day she flew to Manila.

From around the country, news came that more military units were defecting to the mutineers' side. Helicopter gunships that hovered ominously above

Employees at government-owned Channel 4 surrender to rebel forces. Because of the importance of media coverage for the revolution, the television stations were among the first buildings to be captured by the rebels.

the people suddenly landed, and the men inside jumped out waving the opposition "L" sign. On Marcos's orders, Colonel Braulio Balbas had set up a hundred howitzers and cannon across from the main rebel camp. Despite receiving repeated orders from Ver and Marcos to fire, Balbas stalled. He could not bring himself to attack the people surrounding the camp. He saw them not as an impersonal, teeming mass but as fellow Filipinos. Marcos and Ver finally realized that Balbas had to be replaced with someone who would obey orders, but by then they had lost control of the military.

Aquino's flight to Manila was fraught with danger. No one knew if the Philippine air force was still loyal to Marcos and would order all planes to land. Obscure air force orders crackled over the radio. Aquino's plane, however, made it to Manila without incident. Her car then wound cautiously through the streets just as armed military carriers loyal to Marcos rushed toward the scene of the EDSA rebellion. However, no one bothered to look through the car windows to see that the woman whose name the crowd was chanting was right before them.

Aquino reached the safety of a relative's house and contacted Ramos and Enrile. Enrile acknowledged that Marcos had cheated her of the election victory. Now it was time to talk about swearing Aquino in as president. It was crucial that she prove that she, not Enrile, was calling the shots. She demanded that her inauguration ceremony be held at the Club Filipino, an exclusive club in the Greenhills suburb of Manila. The rebel generals arranging security for the inauguration were aghast. "It's within mortar range, and we can't seal it off. It's almost totally indefensible — a tactical nightmare," they protested, trying to convince Aquino to hold the ceremony at the Crame parade ground.

Aquino was adamant. Despite its newly found identity as the rebel headquarters, Crame had for too long been identified as the first place every political detainee under Marcos, including her late husband, was taken. Aquino especially did not want to appear to have come to power in a military coup.

Just outside Malacañang Palace, a young Filipino sells newspapers bearing the latest word on the tense political situation. The rows of barbed wire encircled the palace, where Marcos and his family remained holed up for fear of their lives.

Aquino and Laurel lead a "Victory of the People" protest rally in February 1986. The official government commission, ignoring the blatant election fraud as well as the overwhelming popular vote for Aquino, had declared Marcos the election winner.

On the morning of February 25, 1986, a white Chevrolet van rolled out of a bungalow on Times Street in Quezon City and casually made its way through the throngs that filled the avenues. Few among the crowd paid attention to the car; no one could see through its silver-tinted windows. All eyes were instead focused on the dramatic events taking place a couple of blocks away: Channel 9, a government station, was being contested by Marcos forces and the rebels. Opposition troops fired rounds at government soldiers perched on posts atop the station's transmitting tower. If the rebels captured Channel 9, which continued to air official threats and edicts from Malacañang Palace, they would control practically all broadcast facilities in the capital and rob Marcos of an audience.

The van drove out of Quezon City and into the neighboring municipality of San Juan. Soon, an

escort of Mercedes Benzes attached itself to the Chevrolet. In the Greenhills district of San Juan, helicopter gunships came to the end of their 45-second flight from the nearby military camps of Crame and Aguinaldo. Enrile and Ramos stepped out of the helicopters. Flanked by heavily armed bodyguards, the rebel commanders disappeared into Club Filipino. At the sight of Ramos and Enrile the crowds broke into wild cheers.

Suddenly the van appeared in the distance. The chant that had echoed throughout the islands over the last two months welled up again: "Cory!" A sea of raised arms and yellow banners engulfed the van. By the time it rolled up the club's driveway, the cries were deafening. Corazon Aquino stepped out of the van in a bright yellow dress with embroidered sleeves. She was ready for her inauguration as the seventh president of the Philippines. The ceremony was to be broadcast over Channel 4, the government station rebel troops had captured earlier.

Marcos had planned his own inauguration within Malacañang on the same day, and visitors were streaming into the palace. But the president and his family had become increasingly isolated. The U.S. embassy had adopted a strictly neutral policy. Marcos's friends in Washington were silent. Only a few foreign ambassadors were coming to his inauguration. No Filipino, though, would see Marcos sworn in as president on his last remaining television station. As Marcos stood in front of Channel 9's cameras, rebel soldiers snapped the transmission signal.

After nine o'clock on the evening of February 25, U.S. ambassador Stephen Bosworth called Aquino. Former Supreme Court justice Cecilia Munoz Palma related, "Cool as always, Cory turned to us after she put the phone down. She said simply, 'Marcos has left.' She said it as if it was the most ordinary thing. We all shouted jubilantly." Earlier in the evening, Marcos had fled the palace he had ruled from for 20 years. He took a helicopter to Clark Field, his de-

Corazon Aquino is sworn in as the seventh president of the Republic of the Philippines on February 25, 1986. Marcos held his own inauguration, but the broadcast of the palace ceremony was cut when rebels captured the last remaining government television station.

parture point from the Philippines. Bosworth had relayed to Aquino a request from the former dictator to spend some time in his home province of Ilocos Norte. When her advisers pointed out the possible danger of Marcos setting up a base there, Aquino refused to allow him to stay. In exile in Hawaii, he would continue to scheme but to no avail. He would become a withered, weak old man, always slightly out of touch with reality and increasingly under the control of his erratic wife.

Corazon Aquino was now president of the Philippines. "I cannot help but remember Ninoy," she said in her first speech after the departure of Marcos. "I cannot resist comparing his death to Good Friday and our liberation to Easter Sunday. I am sure that Ninoy is smiling at us now from the life after, for truly we have proved him correct: the Filipino is worth dying for." She ended her speech with the pledge of faith that had sustained her through the death of her husband, the turmoil of the campaign, and the dangers of the last four days of rebellion. Now, at the joyous close of that journey, she focused on the future. She knew she would need strength for the tests that were yet to come, but she was confident. She said to the people, "Our cause is just. God is beside us. We can face the coming trials."

Jubilant Filipinos celebrate the departure of Marcos, who fled the country the night of Aquino's inauguration. Finally convinced by U.S. officials of his defeat, Marcos and his family flew to Hawaii, where they would live in exile.

JANUARY 5, 1987

$1.95

TIME

WOMAN OF THE YEAR

Philippine President Corazon Aquino

7

Queen of Hearts

When Manilans were certain that Marcos had left, they stormed Malacañang Palace in a massive outpouring of the frustration and rage that had been held in for so many years. They looted the palace, destroyed documents and papers, seized weapons, and defaced portraits of the Marcos family before soldiers arrived to restore order. In the following days, ecstatic crowds took apart the old regime's barbed wire in circlets and carried them as crowns of thorns transformed by heroism, and the tiny yellow ribbons attached to them into crowns of glory.

The first act of the new president was an additional act of liberation. Corazon Aquino freed the political prisoners of the dictatorship, the men and women who had suffered just as Benigno had. She abandoned the 1973 constitution Marcos had fashioned for his own purposes and offered peace to the communist guerrillas in the countryside. She said they no longer had any reason to fight on, because the enemy was gone. Corazon Aquino's fairytale rise to power, however, did not automatically come provided with a happy ending. She faced urgent problems that demanded immediate attention.

> *God has a plan for all of us, and it is for each of us to find out what that plan is. I can tell you that I never thought the plan was for me to be President.*
> —CORAZON AQUINO

Corazon Aquino received international acclaim for her peaceful overthrow of the Marcos dictatorship. The new president, however, steadfastly maintained that the victory of the revolution belonged not to her personally, but to the Filipino people, whose strength and faith underlay her own actions.

The Marcoses left behind many possessions, some of which are shown here. When the Aquino forces entered Malacañang Palace, they were stunned to discover the excessive luxury in which the dictator and his wife had lived. The Aquino government turned the palace into a museum.

Her first concern was to consolidate her own power. After the euphoria of the election and revolution subsided, some of Aquino's allies began to desert her, picking at the weaknesses that had been so obscured by the emotion of the campaign: "She has no political experience. How can she run this country?" "She's weak and vacillating. . . . She has no will of her own. She knows nothing." Marcos had been able to decree change. Aquino preferred to reach a democratic consensus. Democracy took too much time, her critics said, and with its many pressing problems, the Philippines did not have time for democracy. The activists in the Muslim minority in the southern Philippines took advantage of the new atmosphere of freedom to demand change and threatened a regional war unless old injustices were righted. Labor unions, long suppressed by Marcos, were taking advantage of the new openness to voice their complaints. With the reinstatement of a free press and freedom of assembly, Filipinos everywhere were speaking their mind. A chaotic whirl of opinions, suggestions, complaints, and demands filled the air.

Some people grew nostalgic for the orderliness of the Marcos regime. Indeed, a few Filipinos remained intensely loyal to the deposed dictator. In August 1986 Marcos's former vice-presidential candidate, Arturo Tolentino, tried to lead a coup against Aquino. Marcos loyalists seized the plush Manila Hotel and proclaimed Tolentino acting president while he awaited the return of Marcos. Without popular backing or military support, the rebellion soon fizzled. But the loyalists would continue to stage violent demonstrations and, later, with money reportedly sent to them from Marcos in Hawaii, they organized terrorist raids in Manila. Marcos vowed to return, but as the months went on the threats became less serious. Although Marcos and his extreme right-wing loyalists would never be in a position to overthrow the new government, they would continue to pester Aquino for a long time.

The most serious threat to Aquino came from Juan Ponce Enrile, whom the new president had appointed defense minister. Soon after joining the Aquino government, Enrile began criticizing the woman whose name had echoed from the throngs that had protected him during the rebellion. He condemned the new administration's slowness to implement a master plan for the nation. He was contemptuous of Aquino's attempts to reach a peaceful agreement with the communists. He opposed the release of those political prisoners he felt still represented a threat to national interests. In particular, he argued against freeing Jose Sison, the Communist party chairman. Soon, the military officers who had conspired with him against Marcos were plotting and spreading rumors that Aquino, who was only in power because the military put her there, was unable to run the country, and that Enrile was better suited to govern.

Enrile, however, grossly underestimated Corazon Aquino. The shy housewife had come into her own during the election campaign. She had learned to use power and influence, and she had a clear conception of the kind of support she had among the people. To them, she was not just another kind of politician; she wielded a personal, moral force that exercised more control over men's actions than had the repressive tactics of the Marcos dictatorship.

As soon as Aquino began to gather the reins of government into her hands, radical groups began to press their own demands. Shown here are members of the Moro National Liberation Front, one of the Muslim separatist groups in the southern Philippines.

Arturo Tolentino, Marcos's former running mate, tried to capitalize on the conflicts that arose in the wake of Aquino's election. In August 1986 Tolentino led a coup attempt against the Aquino government, but he gained little support, and the coup quickly fizzled.

She appealed to the aspirations for good that were in the hearts of all Filipinos. She firmly believed that if anyone tried to force her out of power, she would simply appeal to the people to return to the streets and overwhelm the enemy.

Aquino's relations with the communist rebels remained problematic. After sending representatives to negotiate a peace, the communists demanded a full partnership in a government they had done nothing to bring to power. A month after the revolution, when Aquino assumed comprehensive ruling powers pending the ratification of a new constitution and the election of a responsible legislature, the communists (as well as many other Filipinos) accused her of bringing back a dictatorship. Branding the new president insincere, the guerrillas argued that the people were still impoverished and still oppressed by the rich and the government. The communists thus demanded an immediate and radical land-reform program. Convinced that she needed to develop a just, lasting solution to the formidable problem of land redistribution, Aquino refused to be pushed into immediate, radical action by the communists' charges. She turned down their demands, and the peace talks broke off. The fighting continued, but faced with Aquino's immense popularity and moral force, the communists have been unable to come up with strategies to seriously undermine her administration. Under Marcos, they had demonstrated easily that the head of government was corrupt, but any such allegation against Aquino was not only insulting, it was unbelievable.

This does not mean that there have been no allegations of corruption among her family, friends, and supporters. Any charges made, however, are out in the open and can be publicly debated. Indeed, Aquino's powerful brother Jose, whom many accuse of being too influential with the president, takes some pride in attracting criticism, as long as his sister is not dragged through the mud.

Defense Minister Enrile, whom Aquino retained in his former position, soon became the most vocal critic of her government. His constant opposition to Aquino began to seriously undermine the new president's ability to project an image of confidence and control.

Although some Filipinos still join the insurgents, the communist guerrillas have stopped attracting large numbers. Many have begun to give up armed resistance and to participate in legal political processes. Under Marcos, armed attacks on government officials sometimes had been viewed entirely as the acts of desperate men forced by circumstances to use violence to gain justice. Many viewed the guerrillas as freedom fighters. This is no longer true under the Aquino government. In the eyes of Filipinos desperate for a new age of stability and morality, these acts of violence have become the work of mere terrorists.

From the beginning, international support for President Aquino, especially from the United States, was heartening. In September 1986, Aquino went on a state visit to the United States, despite continued rumors of an Enrile-inspired coup at home. After listening to a stirring speech by the Philippine president, the U.S. Senate approved $200 million in supplemental aid to the Philippines. In November, Japan approved an enormous aid package, larger than the one from the United States. The

One of Aquino's first actions was to open peace talks with the New People's Army. Filipinos who had joined the communists only because no other avenue of political action was open to them began to drift away from the NPA to participate in local political processes.

international community responded very favorably to Aquino's plea for a restructured debt repayment program that would enable the Philippines to deal with its huge foreign debt. "Corymania" took hold around the world: While conferring with the new Philippine president, U.S. secretary of state George Shultz pinned a tiny Corazon Aquino doll on his jacket. Inscribed on it were the words "I Love Cory!"

At home, Aquino maneuvered with great confidence. After returning from her trip to Japan in November 1986, Aquino fired Enrile after giving him enough time to align himself with the loud but unpopular Marcos loyalists, thus discrediting himself among the majority of Filipinos. Furthermore, the military did not rush to Enrile's aid. General Ramos, whom Aquino had appointed chief of staff of the Philippine armed forces, had rallied Filipino officers and soldiers to the cause of military professionalism, insisting on the doctrine of civilian control of the government. Ramos convinced the soldiers that to overthrow the popularly elected government would be wrong. Aquino appointed Rafael Ileto, the deputy defense minister, to Enrile's position.

Marcos supporters, taking advantage of the media freedom allowed by Aquino, agitate for the dictator's return. Many Filipinos feared that Marcos's predictions of anarchy under Aquino would come true and that people would begin to long for the order of Marcos's regime.

In the fall of 1986 Aquino made an official visit to the United States. Her speech to Congress was warmly received and resulted in the granting of a U.S. supplementary aid package worth $200 million.

To prove to both the right and the left that the people were on her side, Aquino campaigned hard for a new constitution that would restrain dictatorial tendencies in future Philippine presidents, as well as assure her of a full six-year term. As the day for the plebiscite on the constitution approached, both sides tried to derail Aquino's campaign. Radicals from both ends of the political spectrum collided in front of Malacañang Palace on January 22, 1987, about a week before the vote was to be held. The radical Farmers' Movement of the Philippines (KMP), protesting that Aquino had reneged on her promise for land reform, held a march. Police and soldiers met the demonstrators at Mendiola Bridge, and when the labor leaders threatened to storm the palace edgy soldiers, perhaps sympathizing with the right, opened fire, killing 12 people. Aquino established a commission to investigate the tragedy.

All the attempts to wreck Aquino's plans only deepened the people's resolve to stick with her. In February 1987, a year after the polls that eventually brought her to power, Corazon Aquino put the new constitution to a vote, and, in the most peaceful election the country had seen in decades, the people approved it by 76 percent. Asked why they voted for the constitution when the country's economic and political problems remained unsolved, many voters said simply, "Cory is different from other leaders we have known. She is good."

The majority understood that Aquino wanted to bring about democracy, and they grew to understand that democracy required time, consensus, and stability. Further proof of the people's trust in their president was their approval of most of the senatorial candidates she supported in the June 1987 congressional elections. Though the elections were not free of violence — few Filipino elections are — irregularities were few. Both the right, led by Enrile, and the left, led by a former NPA commander freed by Aquino, were soundly defeated. Enrile managed to gain a seat in the Senate, but with 22 of 24 seats held by Aquino's coalition, he was part of a very small minority.

Aquino (center) prepares to attend a dinner with U.S. secretary of state George Shultz (who sports an "I Love Cory" doll) and his wife, Helena. Shultz was eager to secure Aquino's support of U.S. interests in the Pacific, especially on the issue of military bases in the Philippines.

Aquino's broad presidential powers ended in July 1987 with the first meeting of the new national legislature. She views the task of government as one of cooperation between herself and the people's representatives to address the immense problems the Philippines still faces. Workable solutions must be found for land reform, the foreign debt, and the problem of the communist insurgents and the Muslim separatists. On the thorny issue of the U.S. bases, Aquino declared her intention to abide by the agreement that keeps them in the Philippines until 1992. Many people have criticized her for this decision, saying that it was a Marcos position she is not obliged to uphold because it undermines Philippine independence and national interests.

British novelist George Orwell wrote that all saints must be presumed guilty until they are found innocent. Corazon Aquino, who has had popular sainthood thrust upon her, was once guilty of mistrusting her own people's courage. But she was raised to power by their belief that innocence and repentance can defeat guile and evil. She is well aware of her responsibilities and of the role she

President Aquino poses for an official portrait with her cabinet. Many of Aquino's early detractors underestimated her political common sense, which was reflected in her solid choices of cabinet members who were committed to Philippine democracy.

must play. In her public life, there is little of the posturing and egotism that characterized Filipino politicos. If Aquino is a politician, she is of a type the Philippines has never before seen. Almost alone among world leaders, she owes her place not to political skills nor to intellectual prowess, but to simple goodness and morality. Aquino became the living symbol of the hopes and the strength of Filipinos.

The story that unfolded in the Philippines in the first two months of 1986 was a morality play of epic proportions. Among the images it produced, the phenomenon of Corazon Aquino stands out. Piang Alabar, a Muslim Filipino, has described the intense meeting of feeling and symbolism most people saw in Aquino's rise to power: "The prophet of Islam has a saying that when one sees an evil or immoral act, one must stop it with his hands. If the evil cannot be stopped with the hands then one must use his tongue. If the tongue cannot stop it, then one must use his heart. . . . The Filipino people stopped Marcos with their tongues and with their heart."

The name *Corazon* means *heart.*

Aquino (center) maintains very close ties with her children, and with her particular style of leadership that sense of family extends to the Filipino people. Aquino's election to the presidency marked the beginning of a new life for her and, she hopes, for the Philippines.

Further Reading

Bonner, Raymond. *Waltzing with a Dictator: The Marcoses and the Making of American Foreign Policy.* New York: Times Books, 1987.

Komisar, Lucy. *Corazon Aquino: The Story of a Revolution.* New York: George Braziller, 1987.

McDougald, Charles C. *The Marcos File.* San Francisco: San Francisco Publishers, 1987.

Mercado, Monina Allarey, ed. *People Power: The Philippine Revolution of 1986.* Manila: The James B. Reuter, S.J., Foundation, 1986.

Pedrosa, Carmen Navarro. *Imelda Marcos: The Rise and Fall of One of the World's Most Powerful Women.* New York: St. Martin's Press, 1987.

Chronology

Jan. 25, 1933	Born Maria Corazon Cojuangco in Paniqui, Tarlac province, the Philippines
1949–1953	Attends Mount St. Vincent College in New York
Oct. 11, 1954	Marries Benigno Servillano Aquino, Jr.
Sept. 1972	Ferdinand Marcos declares martial law; Benigno Aquino arrested and imprisoned
May 1980	Benigno Aquino released to undergo surgery in the United States; Aquino family settles in Newton, Massachusetts
Aug. 21, 1983	Benigno Aquino assassinated upon return to the Philippines
1983–1984	Corazon Aquino participates in opposition demonstrations against Marcos regime
Oct. 1985	Draft Cory Aquino for President Movement begins
Dec. 1985	Aquino declares herself a candidate for president under the Laban coalition
Feb. 7, 1986	Election day; government results show Marcos winner; Aquino charges Marcos with fraud, pledges fight
Feb. 22, 1986	Defense Minister Juan Ponce Enrile and Lt. General Fidel Ramos stage rebellion; Jaime Cardinal Sin calls on people to protect rebels against government attack
Feb. 24, 1986	Under pressure from United States, Marcos and family leave the Philippines
Feb. 25, 1986	Aquino sworn in as 7th president of the Republic of the Philippines
March 25, 1986	Enacts temporary "Freedom Constitution"
June 1, 1986	Constitutional convention begins sessions
July 1986	Pro-Marcos Manila Hotel coup foiled
Sept. 1986	Aquino on state visit to United States
Nov. 1986	Aquino fires Defense Minister Enrile for undermining her government
Feb. 1987	New constitution ratified by vast majority
June 1987	Congressional elections held; Aquino candidates win majority
July 1987	Aquino relinquishes broad presidential powers upon first meeting of national congress

Index

Howard G. Chua-Eoan, a staff writer for *Time* magazine, assisted in *Time*'s coverage of the events leading up to and following the Philippine election that brought Corazon Aquino to power. In this capacity he met with Aquino on several occasions both before and after her rise to the presidency. He also contributed to *Time* when the magazine selected Aquino as its Woman of the Year in 1986. Born in the Philippines, he has lived in the United States since 1979.

Arthur M. Schlesinger, jr., taught history at Harvard for many years and is currently Albert Schweitzer Professor of the Humanities at City University of New York. He is the author of numerous highly praised works in American history and has twice been awarded the Pulitzer Prize. He served in the White House as special assistant to Presidents Kennedy and Johnson.